THE WISDOM OF JOHN PAUL II

Compiled by
Nick Bakalar and Richard Balkin

Introduction by Father John W. White

THE
WISDOM OF

JOHN PAUL II

*The Pope
on Life's Most
Vital Questions*

HarperSanFrancisco
An Imprint of HarperCollins*Publishers*

To Tony and Anne

Sine amicitia vitam esse nullam.
—Cicero

Grateful acknowledgment for permission to reprint previously published material is made to *Libreria Editrice Vaticana.*

THE WISDOM OF JOHN PAUL II: *The Pope on Life's Most Vital Questions.* Copyright © 1995 by Nick Bakalar and Richard Balkin. All rights reserved. Printed in the United States of America. No part of this book may be used or reproduced in any manner whatsoever without written permission except in the case of brief quotations embodied in critical articles and reviews. For information address HarperCollins Publishers, 10 East 53rd Street, New York, NY 10022.

HarperCollins®, 📖®, and HarperSanFrancisco™ are trademarks of HarperCollins Publishers Inc.

Book design by Ralph Fowler. Set in Electra.
FIRST EDITION

Library of Congress Cataloging-in-Publication Data
John Paul II, Pope.
The wisdom of John Paul II : the Pope on life's most vital
questions / compiled by Nick Bakalar & Richard Balkin. — 1st ed.
p.   cm.
Includes bibliographical references.
ISBN 0–06–060474–3 (cloth)
1. Spiritual life—Catholic Church.   2. Church and the world.
3. Catholic Church—Doctrines.   4. Conduct of life.   I. Bakalar,
Nick.   II. Balkin, Richard.   III. Title.
BX2350.2.J638   1995   95–23373
282—dc20   CIP

95 96 97 98 99 ❖HAD 10 9 8 7 6 5 4 3 2 1

Contents

✝

O DIVINE MASTER, GRANT THAT I may not so much seek to be consoled as to console, to be understood as to understand, to be loved as to love; for it is in giving that we receive, it is in pardoning that we are pardoned, and it is in dying that we are born to eternal life.

Speech to Interreligious Leaders at
Los Angeles, September 16, 1987

INTRODUCTION

AFTER NEARLY TWO DECADES AS POPE, THERE SEEMS to be no lessening of interest in Karol Józef Wojtyla, the 262nd successor of St. Peter, the first non-Italian pope in 455 years, and the first Polish pope ever. Indeed, Pope John Paul's fame and popularity seem to keep growing. He is featured on the covers of popular magazines; he has published a bestselling book; his most recent encyclical was front-page news all over the world. And through his worldwide travels, he has been seen by more people than any other person in history.

The Pope is provoking and compelling. As a religious and world leader who has been unafraid to set out before humanity his philosophical and theological understanding of the meaning of human life, he has earned the esteem of people everywhere. By his astounding determination and persistence in carrying out his mission for the soul of humanity and the salvation of the world, he has attracted both dramatic attention and widespread respect. He has undertaken more than sixty trips throughout the world in an effort to awaken faith in anxious hearts at a most uncertain time, and he has touched and stirred the soul of an entire generation of humanity.

This fiercely independent Pope, who makes his own decisions and often goes his own way, has earned high praise even from those who on occasion are disturbed by him. He saddened and angered many, especially the Jewish community, when he accorded the former Austrian president Kurt Waldheim, who has been accused of complicity in Nazi war crimes, a full Vatican reception. Their sadness was compounded when he recognized Waldheim with a papal honor a few years later. On the other hand, many people, and particularly Jewish leaders, were heartened and moved when Pope John Paul prayed in the main synagogue of Rome, the first pope in modern times to do so. John Paul has worked mightily to improve relations with the Jewish community, "our older brothers in the faith."

Within the Catholic community itself, John Paul has also elicited paradoxical responses. Progressive Catholics have been incensed that the Pope frequently selects as heads of major dioceses around the world bishops who are theologically and politically conservative. They also have faulted him for what they call a preoccupation with abortion and sexual ethics. At the same time, these same Catholics cheer the Pope as he speaks out to promote his uncompromising agenda for human rights, world peace, and social development.

Conservative Catholics were dismayed by John Paul's almost daily dramatic denunciations of the Persian Gulf War and, following the war, his strong opposition to continued sanctions against Iraq. More recently, conservatives have been annoyed by the Pope's increasingly vocal and insistent opposition to the use of capital punishment. And yet they applaud him for his efforts to restore the authority of the papacy, for his crackdown on theological dissent, and for his achievements in strengthening Catholic identity.

It is not easy to categorize this Pope and his teachings. He is a profoundly complex thinker, holding two doctorates, one in theology, the other in philosophy. The underpinning of the Pope's theology lies in the twentieth-century school of philosophy called phenomenology, which holds that truth is discovered by experiencing, encountering, and observing it from many perspectives, by "walking around" it and "encircling" it. The Pope, who has "circled" the globe many times during his pontificate, is on an urgent mission to tell the world the truth about God, human existence, and community, and the truth about the solidarity of all peoples. Do not be afraid, the Pope tells us, of the splendor of the truth. It can be said correctly, however contradictory it may seem, that John Paul is at once conservative and liberal, progressive and traditionalist, reactionary and radical.

Most of all, for Pope John Paul II the choice to be made is for God and for solidarity, his new name for love of neighbor. The choice that Christians must make now is for the saving power of the Gospel and for Jesus Christ, the definitive revelation of God's love and truth. It is this choice alone that can create men and women who are led in love and by love and of love, and it is this choice alone that can ultimately yield the holiness on which the future depends.

In response to critics inside the Church who accuse him of abandoning the vision of the Second Vatican Council, the Pope—who was a major participant in the Council—replies that every action of his pontificate has been undertaken in its very spirit and directed to the fulfillment of its challenges. With a tremendous sense of duty and obligation, indeed, as if he came to occupy the See of St. Peter only for this moment, the Pope now prepares the Church in the power of the spirit of the Council for the Third Millennium of Christ and Christianity. Some view the approaching turn of the century with apocalyptic foreboding. Pope John Paul has the opposite perspective. For him, the year 2000 is a Jubilee Year that demands a most sober, serious, and yet profoundly hopeful preparation, and offers the world an enormous opportunity to come together in transformed awareness of our common humanity, sacred dignity, and single destiny. The year 2000 holds for the Church a time of grace, whereby past mistakes and sinfulness are acknowledged and repented. He prays that in these next years the Church, in ways it has never done before, will reclaim its mission of love and service, and in so doing, will hasten the coming of the kingdom of God into this world.

This book represents a broad overview of the Holy Father's thinking, vision, and hopes at this moment in history for the Church and the world. The book is divided into subject categories that grow out of the body of John Paul's teachings and writings, with an editorial headnote introducing each section. The editors offer a representative sample of passages, in the hope of capturing the heart, mind, spirit, and soul of the Pope in his own words.

It has been a privilege to have shared in some small way in this important project. Working with the editors, Nick Bakalar and Rick Balkin, has been a true joy. The time that they devoted to researching the huge wealth of papal materials and the special attention and sensitivity that they have shown in assembling the final selections for inclusion in the collection have been greatly inspiring.

It is a special grace to complete this brief introduction to the words of one of the twentieth century's most important and inspiring human beings, Pope John Paul II, on the occasion of his seventy-fifth birthday.

Father John W. White
New York
May 18, 1995

Note on Citations

The Pope's encyclicals, apostolic exhortations, and letters are cited by name and year. The *Ad Limina* addresses—customary edifying discourses to visiting bishops—which always occur in Rome, are identified by date and by the group of bishops to whom the Pope is speaking. Most of these quotations, however, come from the occasional speeches the Pope gives all over the world. These are cited by date and place, and where it seemed pertinent to the subject, by the audience: workers for speeches on work, youth groups for speeches about young people, the United Nations for certain remarks on human rights, and so on. In addition, where it seemed helpful, we have cited the subject or title of the speech as it appeared in its written form. Many of the Pope's speeches are presented to general audiences in the Vatican, large crowds at sports stadiums, smaller groups at airports, and so on. These speeches are cited by place and date only.

The Wisdom of John Paul II

CONTEMPORARY
SPIRITUALITY

POPE JOHN PAUL CALLS ON CHRISTIANS TO RENEW
their spiritual lives. The Pope insists that just as the body
needs earthly food for growth, the soul needs to drink from the
living waters of the Gospel. Only through tending to both physical and spiritual needs can a person lead a fully integrated life.

John Paul recognizes the value of the awakening of the religious sense in contemporary spiritual movements. These movements, for example, urge a deeper respect for the earth, and
transcend merely rational forms of religion. They awaken the
imagination and religious sensibilities that have been buried
under modern materialism and secularization. But the Pope also
clearly rejects modern forms of spirituality that conflict with the
Gospel message and confuse rather than clarify the human
being's relationship to God.

John Paul emphasizes in particular the centrality of the sacraments of the Eucharist and penance. Christians witness God's love for humankind in the eucharistic meal, and receive God's mercy in the sacrament of penance. Through participation in the sacraments, Christians today deepen their spiritual journeys.

In the race for technological progress, human beings have become estranged from themselves. As a result, they turn to new spiritual movements that attempt to bridge this chasm. Although John Paul believes that the Church can learn from contemporary movements in spirituality, he holds firmly to the past two thousand years of Christian tradition. Christians in the modern world face the challenge of meeting new, complex needs while at the same time holding fast to their biblical heritage.

✠ WHEN INDIVIDUALS AND COMMUNITIES DO
not see a rigorous respect for our moral, cultural and spiritual requirements, based on the dignity of the person and
on the proper identity of each community, beginning with the
family and religious societies, then all the rest—availability of
goods, abundance of technical resources applied to daily life, a
certain level of material well-being—will prove unsatisfying and
in the end contemptible.

Encyclical: On Social Concerns (Sollicitudo Rei Socialis), 1987

✠ DEVELOPMENT WHICH IS MERELY ECONOMIC
is incapable of setting man free; on the contrary, it will
end by enslaving him further. Development that does not
include the *cultural, transcendent and religious dimensions* of
man and society, to the extent that it does not recognize the existence of such dimensions and does not endeavor to direct its goals
and priorities toward the same, is *even less* conducive to authentic
liberation. Human beings are totally free only when they are
completely *themselves*, in the fullness of their rights and duties.
The same can be said about society as a whole.

Encyclical: On Social Concerns (Sollicitudo Rei Socialis), 1987

✠ THE DISCIPLE OF CHRIST IS CONSTANTLY
challenged by a spreading "practical atheism"—an indifference to God's loving plan which obscures the religious
and moral sense of the human heart. Many either think and act
as if God did not exist or tend to "privatize" religious belief and
practice, so that there exists a bias toward indifferentism and the
elimination of any real reference to binding truths and moral

values. When the basic principles which inspire and direct human behavior are fragmentary and even at times contradictory, society increasingly struggles to maintain harmony and a sense of its own destiny. In a desire to find some common ground on which to build its programs and policies, it tends to restrict the contribution of those whose moral conscience is formed by their religious beliefs.

Ad Limina *Address to Bishops*
from New Jersey and Pennsylvania, November 11, 1993

✠ THE CHURCH FEELS THE DUTY TO PROCLAIM the liberation of millions of human beings, the duty to help this liberation become firmly established; but she also feels the corresponding duty to proclaim liberation in its integral and profound meanings, as Jesus proclaimed and realized it. Liberation made up of reconciliation and forgiveness. Liberation springing from the reality of being children of God, whom we are able to call Abba, Father (Rom 8:15), a reality which makes us recognize in every man a brother of ours, capable of being transformed in his heart through God's mercy. Liberation that, with the energy of love, urges us toward fellowship, the summit and fullness of which we find in the Lord. Liberation as the overcoming of the various forms of slavery and man-made idols, and as the growth of the new man. Liberation that in the framework of the Church's proper mission is not reduced to the simple and narrow economic, political, social or cultural dimension, and is not sacrificed to the demands of any strategy, practice or short-term solution.

Address at Puebla to Latin American Bishops, January 28, 1979

✠ IT IS NOT AN EXAGGERATION TO SAY THAT man's relationship to God and the demand for a religious "experience" are the crux of a profound crisis affecting the human spirit. While the secularization of many aspects of life continues, there is a new quest for "spirituality" as evidenced in the appearance of many religious and healing movements which look to respond to the crisis of values in Western society. This stirring of the *homo religiosus* produces some positive and constructive results, such as the search for new meaning in life, a new ecological sensitivity and the desire to go beyond a cold, rationalistic religiosity. On the other hand, this religious reawakening includes some very ambiguous elements which are incompatible with the Christian faith.

Beyond New Age Ideas: Spiritual Renewal
Ad Limina *Address to U.S. Bishops, May 28, 1993*

✠ MODERN RATIONALISM DOES NOT TOLERATE mystery. It does not accept the mystery of man as male and female nor is it willing to admit that the full truth about man has been revealed in Jesus Christ. In particular, it does not accept the great mystery proclaimed in the Letter to the Ephesians, but radically opposes it. It may well acknowledge, in the context of a vague deism, the possibility and even the need for a supreme or divine being, but it firmly rejects the idea of a God who became man in order to save man. For rationalism it is unthinkable that God should be the redeemer, much less that He should be the bridegroom, the primordial and unique source of the human love between spouses. Rationalism provides a radically different way of looking at creation and the meaning of human existence. But once man begins to lose sight of a God who loves him, a God who calls man through Christ to live in Him and with Him, and once the family no longer has the possibility of sharing in the great mystery, what is left except the mere temporal dimension of life? Earthly life becomes nothing more than the scenario of a battle for existence, of a desperate search for gain, and financial gain before all else.

Letter to Families for the International Year of the Family,
February 22, 1994

✠ TO MANY PEOPLE, MERCY AND CONVERSION may seem like poor tools for solving social problems. Some are tempted to accept ideologies that use force to carry out their programs and impose their vision. Such means sometimes produce what appear to be successes. But these successes are not real. Force and manipulation have nothing to do with true human development and the defense of human dignity. Catholic social teaching is totally different, not only as regards goals, but also as regards the means to be used. For the Christian, putting right human ills must necessarily take into account the reality of creation and redemption. It means treating every human being as a unique child of God, a brother or sister of Jesus Christ. The path of human solidarity is the path of service; and true service means selfless love, open to the needs of all, without distinction of persons, with the explicit purpose of reinforcing each person's sense of God-given dignity.

Address to Catholic Charities, California, September 13, 1987

✠ THE SEPARATION OF SPIRIT AND BODY IN MAN has led to a growing tendency to consider the human body, not in accordance with the categories of its specific likeness to God, but rather on the basis of its similarity to all the other bodies present in the world of nature, bodies which man uses as raw material in his efforts to produce goods for consumption. But everyone can immediately realize what enormous dangers lurk behind the application of such criteria to man. When the human body, considered apart from spirit and thought, comes to be used as raw material in the same way that bodies of animals are used—and this actually occurs for example in experimentation on embryos and fetuses—we will inevitably arrive at a dreadful ethical defeat.

Letters to Families for the International Year of the Family, February 22, 1994.

✠ A FEW YEARS AGO, THERE WAS MUCH TALK OF the secularized world, the post-Christian era. Fashion changes, but a profound reality remains. Christians today must be formed to live in a world which largely ignores God or which, in religious matters, in place of an exacting and fraternal dialogue, stimulating for all, too often founders in a debasing indifferentism, if it does not remain in a scornful attitude of "suspicion" in the name of the progress it has made in the field of scientific "explanations." To "hold on" in this world, to offer to all a "dialogue of salvation" in which each person feels respected in his or her most basic dignity, the dignity of one who is seeking God, we need a catechesis which trains the young people and adults of our communities to remain clear and consistent in their faith, to affirm serenely their Christian and Catholic identity, to "see him who is invisible" and to adhere so firmly to the absoluteness of God that they can be witnesses to Him in a materialistic civilization that denies Him.

Catechesis in Our Time, October 1979

HUMAN RIGHTS

IN HIS WORLD TRAVELS, POPE JOHN PAUL HAS TAKEN a very direct approach to governments that do not live up to basic standards of human rights. While visiting Buenos Aires he referred directly to the Argentinian government's "dirty war," and pointedly held a meeting with one of the few bishops in the country who had spoken out against the government. In Africa, in 1985, he made a direct appeal to President Mobutu of Zaire, and condemned South Africa's apartheid. In South Korea, he spoke both publicly and privately with the president about the need for greater democracy and greater respect for personal liberty. No government is spared: the Holy Father has condemned equally governments of the left and the right for what he perceives as violations of human rights.

There is little question that the Pope's urgings have had practical effect. Mikhail Gorbachev has given the Holy Father much credit for the liberalization of Eastern Europe, and Lech Walesa has acknowledged the Pope's aid as essential in preserving the gains of Solidarity in Poland.

Pope John Paul's campaign for human rights has always emphasized that social justice cannot be accomplished through class hatred or violence. In poor countries around the world, he has reminded the wealthy that their security cannot be bought at the expense of violations of the rights of the poor, and that redistribution of land, under certain circumstances, is a proper response to exploitation. If John Paul is a traditionalist in theological matters, he has not hesitated to advocate radical solutions to social problems.

HUMAN RIGHTS

✠ THE CHRISTIAN VIEW IS THAT HUMAN BEINGS
are to be valued for what they are, not for what they have.
In loving the poor and serving those in whatever need, the
Church seeks above all to respect and heal their human dignity.
The aim of Christian solidarity and service is to defend and promote, in the name of Jesus Christ, the dignity and fundamental
human rights of every person. The Church bears witness to the
fact that this dignity cannot be destroyed, whatever the situation
of poverty, scorn, rejection or powerlessness to which a human
being has been reduced. She shows her solidarity with those who
do not count in a society by which they are rejected spiritually
and sometimes even physically.

Address at San Antonio, September 13, 1987

✠ THE DEPRESSED RURAL WORLD, THE WORKER
who, with his sweat, waters also his affliction, cannot wait
any longer for full and effective recognition of his dignity,
which is not inferior to that of any other social sector.

Address to Indians and Peasants at Cuilapa, Mexico,
January 29, 1979

✠ AND HOW CAN WE FAIL TO CONSIDER THE
violence against life done to millions of human beings, especially children, who are forced into poverty, malnutrition and hunger because of an unjust distribution of resources
between peoples and between social classes? And what of the violence inherent not only in wars as such, but in the scandalous
arms trade, which spawns the many armed conflicts which stain
our world with blood? What of the spreading of death caused by

reckless tampering with the world's ecological balance, by the criminal spread of drugs or by the promotion of certain kinds of sexual activity which, besides being morally unacceptable, also involve grave risks to life? It is impossible to catalogue completely the vast array of threats to human life, so many are the forms, whether explicit or hidden, in which they appear today!

Encyclical: The Gospel of Life (Evangelium Vitae), *1995*

MOREOVER, IF IT IS PROPERLY UNDERSTOOD, religious freedom will help to ensure the order and common welfare of each nation, of each society, for, when individuals know that their fundamental rights are protected, they are better prepared to work for the common welfare.

The Freedom of Conscience and Religions, September 1, 1980

YOU HAVE RECEIVED, DEAR INDIGENOUS brothers and sisters of America, a rich heritage of human wisdom and at the same time you have been entrusted with your peoples' hopes for the future. The Church, on her part, openly affirms every Christian's right to his own cultural heritage, as something inherent in his dignity as a person and child of God. In its authentic values of truth, goodness and beauty, this heritage must be recognized and respected. Unfortunately, we must admit that the richness of your cultures has not always been appreciated nor have your rights as individuals and peoples been respected. The shadow of sin was cast over America too in the destruction of many of your artistic and cultural creations and in the violence to which you were often subjected.

Address in Mexico to Native Peoples, August 11, 1993

EVERY HUMAN PERSON — NO MATTER HOW vulnerable or helpless, no matter how young or how old, no matter how healthy, handicapped or sick, no matter how useful or productive for society—is a being of inestimable worth created in the image and likeness of God. This is the dignity of America, the reason she exists, the condition for her survival—yes, the ultimate test of her greatness: to respect every human person, especially the weakest and most defenseless ones, those as yet unborn.

Address at Detroit Airport, September 19, 1987

✠ ON THIS MATTER [THE DEATH PENALTY] there is a growing tendency, both in the Church and in civil society, to demand that it be applied in a very limited way, or even that it be abolished completely. The nature and extent of the punishment must be carefully evaluated and decided upon, and ought not go to the extreme of executing the offender except in cases of absolute necessity: in other words, when it would not be possible otherwise to defend society. Today, however, as a result of steady improvements in the organization of the penal system, such cases are very rare if not practically nonexistent.

Encyclical: The Gospel of Life
(Evangelium Vitae), *1995*

✠ THE UNIVERSAL DECLARATION OF HUMAN Rights—with its train of many declarations and conventions on highly important aspects of human rights, in favor of children, of women, of equality between races, and especially the two international covenants on economic, social and cultural rights and on civil and political rights—must remain the basic value in the United Nations organization with which the consciences of its members must be confronted and from which they must draw continual inspiration. If the truths and principles contained in this document were to be forgotten or ignored and were thus to lose the genuine self-evidence that distinguished them at the time they were brought painfully to birth, then the noble purpose of the United Nations organization could be faced with the threat of a new destruction.

Address to the United Nations, October 2, 1979

✠ FROM THE THEOLOGICAL POINT OF VIEW EVERY baptized person, precisely by reason of being baptized, has the right to receive from the Church instruction and education enabling him or her to enter on a truly Christian life; and from the viewpoint of human rights, every human being has the right to seek religious truth and adhere to it freely, that is to say, "without coercion on the part of individuals or of social groups and any human power," in such a way that in this matter of religion, "no one is to be forced to act against his or her conscience or prevented from acting in conformity to it."

Catechesis in Our Time, October 1979

✠ INSTITUTIONS AND LAWS UNJUSTLY IGNORE the inviolable right of the family and of the human person; and society, far from putting itself at the service of the family, attacks it violently in its values and fundamental requirements. Thus the family, which in God's plan is the basic cell of society and a subject of rights and duties before the state or any other community, finds itself the victim of society, of the delays and slowness with which it acts, and even of its blatant injustice.

For this reason, the Church openly and strongly defends the rights of the family against the intolerable usurpations of society and the state.

Apostolic Exhortation Familiaris Consortio, 1981

✠ EVEN IN EXCEPTIONAL SITUATIONS THAT MAY at times arise, one can never justify any violation of the fundamental dignity of the human person or of the basic rights that safeguard this dignity. Legitimate concern for the security of a nation, as demanded by the common good, could lead to the temptation of subjugating to the state the human being and his or her dignity and rights. Any apparent conflict between the exigencies of security and of the citizens' basic rights must be resolved according to the fundamental principle—upheld always by the Church—that social organization exists only for the service of man and for the protection of his dignity, and that it cannot claim to serve the common good when human rights are not safeguarded.

Address at Manila, February 17, 1980

THE LAITY

POPE JOHN PAUL II EMBRACES THE SPIRIT OF VATI-can II when he addresses the role of the laity in the Church today. He encourages lay men and women to take on more responsibilities in the various ministries of the Church. The world encounters the Church through the laity in a distinctive way. Armed with the Living Word, the laity are called to live out their faith in both their Church and their secular communities.

The Pope believes that lay people are vital to the mission of the Church. He encourages them to partake actively in the liturgical, educational, and social life of their communities. Through full participation in parish life, lay men and women nourish their brothers and sisters, witnessing the Gospel ideal of faithful service to others. Their efforts as religious educators, eucharistic ministers, pastoral counselors, and diocesan administrators build up the Living Body of Christ. Through the laity, the Church ministers more fully to the complex needs of the faithful.

In secular society, the laity bear witness to the reality of Christ and "permeate [society] with the leaven of the Gospel." In their social, political, intellectual, and economic pursuits, the laity are challenged to imitate Christ. They are called to fulfill a mission: to bring spiritual values to secular life.

John Paul II writes that as "citizens of both the earthly city and the heavenly kingdom," lay Catholics participate in the mission of the Church by receiving the holy sacraments and embodying the message of the Gospel in the world. The laity who respond to this vocation provide an irreplaceable service to the Church and the world.

THE LAITY

✠ THE ROLE OF LAY PEOPLE IN THE MISSION OF the Church extends in two directions: in union with your pastors and assisted by their guidance you build up the communion of the faithful; second, as responsible citizens you permeate with the leaven of the Gospel the society in which you live, in its economic, social, political, cultural and intellectual dimension. When you faithfully carry out these two roles as citizens of both the earthly city and the heavenly kingdom, then are the words of Christ fulfilled: "You are the salt of the earth. . . . You are the light of the world" (Mt 5:13–14).

Homily at Accra, Ghana, May 8, 1980

✠ IT IS [THE LAITY'S] SPECIFIC VOCATION AND mission to express the Gospel in their lives and thereby to insert the Gospel as a leaven into the reality of the world in which they live and work. The great forces which shape the world—politics, the mass media, science, technology, culture, education, industry and work—are precisely the areas where lay people are especially competent to exercise their mission. If these forces are guided by people who are true disciples of Christ and who are, at the same time, fully competent in the relevant secular knowledge and skill, then indeed will the world be transformed from within by Christ's redeeming power.

Homily in County Limerick, October 1, 1979

✠ THE DEVELOPMENT IN THE UNITED STATES OF what is commonly called lay ministry is certainly a positive and fruitful result of the renewal begun by the Second Vatican Council. Particular attention needs to be paid to the spiritual and doctrinal formation of all lay ministers. In every case they should be men and women of faith, exemplary in personal and family life, who lovingly embrace "the full and complete proclamation of the good news" (*Reconciliatio et Paenitentia*, 9) taught by the Church.

On Parishes, Lay Ministry, and Women's Roles
Ad Limina *Address to the U.S. Bishops of*
Baltimore, Washington, Atlanta, and Miami,
July 2, 1993

✠ PARTICULAR CARE MUST BE GIVEN TO FORMING a social conscience at all levels and in all sectors. When injustices worsen and the distance between rich and poor increases distressingly, the social doctrine, in a form which is creative and open to the broad fields of the Church's presence, must be a valuable instrument for formation and action. This holds good particularly for the laity: "It is to the laity, though not exclusively to them, that secular duties and activity properly belong" (*Gaudium et Spes*, 43). It is necessary to avoid supplanting the laity and to study seriously just when certain forms of assistance to them retain their reason for existence. Is it not the laity who are called, by reason of their vocation in the Church, to make their contribution in the political and economic dimensions, and to be effectively present in the safeguarding and advancement of human rights?

Address at Puebla to Latin American Bishops, January 28, 1979

✠ THE MISSION OF THE CHURCH IN THE WORLD is accomplished not only by ministers who have received the sacrament of orders, but also by all the lay faithful. Because they have been baptized, the lay faithful share in the priestly, prophetic and royal functions of Christ.

Address at Réunion, May 30, 1989

✠ YOUR CHRISTIAN VOCATION DOES NOT TAKE
  you away from any of your other brothers and sisters. It
  does not inhibit your involvement in civic affairs nor ex-
empt you from your responsibilities as a citizen. It does not divide
you from society nor relieve you of the daily trials of life. Rather
your continued engagement in secular activities and professions
is truly a part of your vocation. For you are called to make the
Church present and fruitful in the ordinary circumstances of
life—in married and family life, in the daily conditions of earning
a living, in political and civic responsibilities and in cultural, scientific and educational pursuits. No human activity is foreign to
the Gospel. God wishes all of creation to be ordered to His kingdom, and it is especially to the laity that the Lord has entrusted
this task.

Homily at Accra, Ghana, May 8, 1980

✠ TO PERFORM A CHURCH CALLING AS LAY MEN
  and women often means giving clear witness to the
  Church against the customary social habits of ordinary living. It means having to bring the demands of the Church calling,
the demands of the family and the demands of one's personal life
into harmony. You can achieve this through living more con-
sciously from the springs of your life, by the Holy Spirit, the
springs which you received in your baptism and confirmation.

Address to Lay Church Workers, West Germany, November 18, 1980

✠ YOU WHO ARE LAY PERSONS IN THE CHURCH
  and who possess faith, the greatest of all resources—you
  have a unique opportunity and crucial responsibility.
Through your lives in the midst of your daily activities in the
world, you show the power that faith has to transform the world
and to renew the family of man.

Homily at Accra, Ghana, May 8, 1980

✠ IT IS A BLESSING FOR THE CHURCH THAT IN
so many parishes the lay faithful assist priests in a variety of
ways: in religious education, pastoral counseling, social
service activities, administration, etc. This increased participation is undoubtedly a work of the Spirit renewing the Church's
vigor.

On Parishes, Lay Ministry, and Women's Roles
Ad Limina *Address to the U.S. Bishops of*
Baltimore, Washington, Atlanta, and Miami, July 2, 1993

✠ AS MEMBERS OF THE LAITY, YOU ARE CALLED
to take an active part in the sacramental and liturgical life
of the Church, especially in the eucharistic sacrifice. At
the same time you are called to spread the Gospel actively
through the practice of charity and through involvement in cate-
chetical and missionary efforts, according to the gifts which each
one of you has received (cf. 1 Cor 12:4ff.).

Homily at Accra, Ghana, May 8, 1980

✠ THE CHRISTIAN FAITH DOES NOT PROVIDE YOU
with ready-made solutions to the complex problems affecting contemporary society. But it does give you deep insights into the nature of man and his needs, calling you to speak
the truth in love, to take up your responsibilities as good citizens
and to work with your neighbors to build a society where true
human values are nourished and deepened by a shared Christian
vision of life.

Homily at Nairobi, Kenya, May 7, 1980

LOVE

ALTHOUGH JOHN PAUL AFFIRMS THAT HUMAN EROTIC impulses are a gift of God, they are nevertheless not the basis for love. Love must be a true gift of the self to another, and cannot be based on the selfishness implied in the mere satisfaction of sexual desire. John Paul does not reject erotic delight, but he does condemn lust—false eroticism—as the attraction toward a partial good instead of toward the complete value of another person created in the image of God. He also encourages self-restraint in resisting impulses that arise from mere carnality because acts based on such impulses are devoid of conscious choice.

We are images of God not only in our minds and spirit, but in our physical bodies as well. John Paul affirms that the human body and its sexual drives are potentially good, and an individual among other individuals finds his way to God either through the responsible love of another in marriage or by being called to practice celibacy and uphold virginity.

John Paul emphasizes that real love is difficult and demanding, and that love—between men and women, parents and children, friends, even between nations and peoples—requires self-sacrifice and self-discipline. In the end, however, love is richly rewarded with joy.

LOVE

✠ MAN CANNOT LIVE WITHOUT LOVE. HE REMAINS a being that is incomprehensible for himself, his life is senseless, if love is not revealed to him, if he does not encounter love, if he does not experience it and make it his own, if he does not participate intimately in it. This, as has already been said, is why Christ the Redeemer "fully reveals man to himself." If we may use the expression, this is the human dimension of the mystery of the Redemption.

Encyclical: The Redeemer of Man (Redemptor Hominis), 1979

✠ ALTHOUGH EVERYTHING SEEMS TO CONFIRM that love is a thing "of the world," that it is born in souls and bodies as the fruit of emotional sensitivity and sensuous attraction, reaching to the hidden depths of the sexual constitution of the organism, yet through all this and as if over and above all this, love is a gift.

Fruitful and Responsible Love, 1979

✠ ABOVE ALL, HOLD HIGH THE ESTEEM FOR THE wonderful dignity and grace of the sacrament of marriage. Prepare earnestly for it. Believe in the spiritual power which this sacrament of Jesus Christ gives to strengthen the marriage union and to overcome all the crises and problems of life together.

Married people must believe in the power of the sacrament to make them holy. They must believe in their vocation to witness through their marriage to the power of Christ's love. True love and the grace of God can never let marriage become a self-centered relationship of two individuals, living side by side for their own interests.

Homily at County Limerick, Ireland,
October 1, 1979

✠ WITHIN THIS SAME CULTURAL CLIMATE, THE body is no longer perceived as a properly personal reality, a sign and place of relations with others, with God and with the world. It is reduced to pure materiality: it is simply a complex of organs, functions and energies to be used according to the sole criteria of pleasure and efficiency. Consequently, sexuality too is depersonalized and exploited: from being the sign, place and language of love, that is, of the gift of self and acceptance of another in all the other's richness as a person, it increasingly becomes the occasion and instrument for self-assertion and the selfish satisfaction of personal desires and instincts. Thus the original import of human sexuality is distorted and falsified, and the two meanings, unitive and procreative, inherent in the very nature of the conjugal act are artificially separated: in this way the marriage union is betrayed and its fruitfulness is subjected to the caprice of the couple.

Encyclical: The Gospel of Life (Evangelium Vitae), 1995

✠ THE CENTRAL VALUE, UPON WHICH OTHER values in love depend, is the value of the human person. It is to the human person that basic responsibility refers. The texts of the Second Vatican Council affirm many times that love in general, and conjugal love in particular, consists in the gift of one person to another, a gift that embraces the human being as a whole, soul and body. Such a gift presupposes that the person as such has a unique value for the other person, which expresses itself in a particular responsibility for that value, precisely because of its degree and because of its intensity, so to speak. And through a responsibility thus conceived there is formed the essential structure of marriage, a bond at once spiritual and moral.

Fruitful and Responsible Love, 1979

✝ SO OFTEN THE PRESSURES OF MODERN LIVING separate husbands and wives from one another, threatening their lifelong interdependence of love and fidelity. Can we also not be concerned about the impact of cultural pressures upon relations between the generations, upon parental authority and the transmission of sacred values? Our Christian conscience should be deeply concerned about the way in which sins against love and against life are often presented as examples of "progress" and emancipation. Most often, are they not but the age-old forms of selfishness dressed up in a new language and presented in a new cultural framework?

Building Up the Body of Christ
Pastoral Visit to the United States, 1987

✝ IN FACT IT IS ONE THING TO BE CONSCIOUS that the value of sex is a part of all the rich storehouse of values with which the female appears to the male; it is another to "reduce" all the personal riches of femininity to that single value, that is, as a suitable object of gratification of sexuality itself. The same reasoning can be valid concerning what masculinity is for the woman.

Blessed Are the Pure of Heart
General Audience, September 17, 1980

✝ CONJUGAL LOVE IS FULFILLED BY PARENTHOOD. Responsibility for this love from the beginning to the end is at the same time responsibility also for parenthood. The one participates in the other, and they both constitute each other.

Parenthood is a gift that comes to people, to man and to woman, together with love, that creates a perspective of love in the dimension of a reciprocal lifelong self-giving, and that is the condition of gradual realization of that perspective through life and action.

Fruitful and Responsible Love, 1979

✝ REAL LOVE IS DEMANDING. I WOULD FAIL IN my mission if I did not clearly tell you so. For it was Jesus—our Jesus Himself—who said, "You are my friends if you do what I command you" (Jn 15:14). Love demands effort and a personal commitment to the will of God. It means discipline and sacrifice, but it also means joy and human fulfillment.

Address at Boston, October 1, 1979

✝ THE MESSAGE OF LOVE THAT CHRIST BROUGHT is always important, always relevant. It is not difficult to see how today's world, despite its beauty and grandeur, despite the conquests of science and technology, despite the refined and abundant material good that it offers, is yearning for more truth, for more love, for more joy. And all of this is found in Christ and His way of life.

Address at Boston, October 1, 1979

MARRIAGE AND THE FAMILY

FOR JOHN PAUL, THE ESSENTIAL MISSION OF THE family is to create an atmosphere in which love can flourish. In this, the family imitates the bond of love that ties Christ to the members of the Church. In fact, the family is a church in miniature, a domestic church with its own mission.

John Paul sees two opposing forces at work today that affect the family. On the one hand, there is a greater attempt to ensure personal freedom and examine the quality of relationships, which includes assuring the dignity and equality of women and children. On the other, he notices a disturbing degradation of some fundamental values: mistaken ideas of the meaning of individual freedom of the spouses, confusion about the authority of parents over children, and an increase in divorce and abortion.

The Holy Father urges Catholics to use the family as the first school of social life, an example of how to live in the broader community; and he specifically instructs families to dedicate themselves to social service, especially on behalf of the poor. He reminds parents that these activities should involve the children as well, each in the measure that age and ability allow them to participate.

Parents are the first and most important educators of their children, and this is a role they can never abdicate. Children need acceptance, love, esteem, spiritual and emotional support, and also the material resources that make healthy childhood possible. Nor can the elderly be forgotten, and John Paul observes that certain nonindustrial cultures do much better than some in the industrial world in assuring the elderly a proper and dignified place in the life of the family.

MARRIAGE AND THE FAMILY

✠ THE BOND THAT UNITES A FAMILY IS NOT ONLY
a matter of natural kinship or of shared life and experience. It is essentially a holy and religious bond. Marriage
and the family are sacred realities.

> *Building Up the Body of Christ*
> *Pastoral Visit to the United States, 1987*

✠ THE FAMILY IS *THE FIRST SETTING OF*
evangelization, the place where the Good News of Christ
is first received, and then, in simple yet profound ways
handed on from generation to generation. At the same time, families in our time finally depend upon the Church to defend their
rights and to teach the obligations and responsibilities which lead
to the fullness of joy and life. Thus, I urge all of you, especially
the clergy, to teach the obligations and responsibilities which
lead to the fullness of joy and life. Thus, I urge all of you, especially the clergy and the Religious, to work for the promotion of
family values within the local community.

> *Address at New Orleans, September 12, 1987*

✠ GIVING LIFE AND HELPING THEIR CHILDREN TO
reach maturity through education are among the primary
privileges and responsibilities of married couples. We
know that married couples usually look forward to parenthood
but are sometimes impeded from achieving their hopes and desires by social conditions, by personal circumstances or even by
inability to beget life. But the Church encourages couples to be
generous and hopeful, to realize that parenthood is a privilege

and that each child bears witness to the couple's own love for each other, to their generosity and to their openness to God. They must be encouraged to see the child as an enrichment of their marriage and a gift of God to themselves and to their other children.

Ad Limina *Address to U.S. Bishops, September 24, 1983*

CHRISTIAN FAMILIES EXIST TO FORM A communion of persons in love. As such, the Church and the family are each in its own way living representations in human history of the eternal loving communion of the three persons of the Most Holy Trinity. In fact, the family is called the Church in miniature, "the domestic church," a particular expression of the Church through the human experience of love and common life.

Address at Columbia, South Carolina, September 11, 1987

ACCEPTANCE, LOVE, ESTEEM, MANY-SIDED and united material, emotional, educational and spiritual concern for every child that comes into this world should always constitute a distinctive, essential characteristic of all Christians, in particular of the Christian family: thus children, while they are able to grow "in wisdom and in stature, and in favor with God and man," offer their own precious contribution to building up the family community and even to the sanctification of their parents.

Apostolic Exhortation Familiaris Consortio, 1981

THE FAMILY IS SET AT THE VERY CENTER OF common good in its various dimensions, precisely because man is conceived and born in it. Everything possible must be done in order that this human being may be desired, awaited, experienced as a particular, unique and unrepeatable value, right from the beginning, from the moment of his conception. He must feel that he is important, useful, dear and of great value, even if infirm or handicapped; even dearer in fact for this reason.

The Family: Center of Love and Life
General Audience, January 3, 1979

✠ THE DOMESTIC VIRTUES, BASED UPON A profound respect for human life and dignity, and practiced in understanding, patience, mutual encouragement and forgiveness, enable the community of the family to live out the first and fundamental experience of peace.

The Family Creates the Peace of the Human Family
World Day of Peace Message, January 1, 1994

✠ THE PHARAOH OF OLD, HAUNTED BY THE presence and increase of the children of Israel, submitted them to every kind of oppression and ordered that every male child born of the Hebrew women was to be killed (cf. Ex 1:7–22). Today, not a few of the powerful of the earth act in the same way. They too are haunted by the current demographic growth and fear that the most prolific and poorest peoples represent a threat to the well-being and peace of their own countries. Consequently, rather than wishing to face and solve these serious problems with respect for the dignity of individuals and families and for every person's inviolable right to life, they prefer to promote and impose by whatever means a massive program of birth control. Even the economic help which they would be ready to give is unjustly made conditional on the acceptance of antibirth policy.

Encyclical: The Gospel of Life (Evangelium Vitae), 1995

✠ CHRISTIAN MARRIAGE, LIKE THE OTHER sacraments, "whose purpose is to sanctify people, to build up the body of Christ, and finally, to give worship to God," is in itself a liturgical action glorifying God in Jesus Christ and in the Church. By celebrating it, Christian spouses profess their gratitude to God for the sublime gift bestowed on them of being able to live in their married and family lives the very love of God for people and that of the Lord Jesus for the Church, His bride.

Apostolic Exhortation Familiaris Consortio, 1981

✠ I HAVE SPOKEN OF TWO CLOSELY RELATED YET not identical concepts: the concept of communion and that of community. Communion has to do with the personal relationship between the I and the thou. Community, on the other hand, transcends this framework and moves toward a society, a we. The family, as a community of persons, is thus the first human society. It arises whenever there comes into being the conjugal covenant of marriage, which opens the spouses to a lasting communion of love and of life, and it is brought to completion in a full and specific way with the procreation of children: the communion of the spouses gives rise to the community of the family. The community of the family is completely pervaded by the very essence of communion. On the human level, can there by any other communion comparable to that between a mother and a child whom she has carried in her womb and then brought to birth?

Letter to Families for the International Year of the Family, February 22, 1994

✠ IN ORDER THAT CHRISTIAN MARRIAGE MAY favor the total good and development of the married couple, it must be inspired by the Gospel, and thus be open to new life—new life to be given and accepted generously. The couple is also called to create a family atmosphere in which children can be happy and lead full and worthy human and Christian lives.

Homily at the Washington Mall, October 7, 1979

✠ EXPERIENCE TEACHES THAT HUMAN LOVE, which naturally tends toward fatherhood and motherhood, is sometimes affected by a profound crisis and is thus seriously threatened. In such cases help can be sought at marriage and family counseling centers where it is possible, among other things, to obtain the assistance of specifically trained psychologists and psychotherapists. At the same time, however, we cannot forget the perennial validity of the words of the apostle: "I bow my knees before the Father, from whom every family in heaven and on earth is named." Marriage, the sacrament of matrimony, is a covenant of persons in love. And love can be deepened and preserved only by love, that love which is "poured into our hearts through the Holy Spirit which has been given to us" (Rom 5:5).

Letter to Families for the International Year of the Family,
February 22, 1994

✠ IN THE CONVICTION THAT THE GOOD OF THE family is an indispensable and essential value of the civil community, the public authorities must do everything possible to ensure that families have all those aids—economic, social, educational, political and cultural assistance—that they need in order to face all their responsibilities in a human way.

Apostolic Exhortation Familiaris Consortio, *1981*

✠ AUTHENTIC CONJUGAL LOVE PRESUPPOSES and requires that a man have a profound respect for the equal dignity of his wife: "You are not her master," writes St. Ambrose, "but her husband; she was not given to you to be your slave, but your wife. . . . Reciprocate her attentiveness to you and be grateful to her for her love." With his wife a man should live "a very special form of personal friendship." As for the Christian, he is called upon to develop a new attitude of love, manifesting toward his wife a charity that is both gentle and strong like that which Christ has for the Church.

Apostolic Exhortation Familiaris Consortio, 1981

✠ SEXUALITY, BY MEANS OF WHICH MAN AND woman give themselves to one another through the acts which are proper and exclusive to spouses, is by no means something purely biological, but concerns the innermost being of the human person as such. It is realized in a truly human way only if it is an integral part of the love by which a man and a woman commit themselves totally to one another until death.

Apostolic Exhortation Familiaris Consortio, 1981

✠ THE CHURCH CONDEMNS AS A GRAVE OFFENSE against human dignity and justice all those activities of governments or other public authorities which attempt to limit in any way the freedom of couples in deciding about children. Consequently, any violence applied by such authorities in favor of contraception or, still worse, of sterilization and procured abortion must be altogether condemned and forcefully rejected. Likewise to be denounced as gravely unjust are cases where in international relations economic help given for the advancement of peoples is made conditional on programs of contraception, sterilization and procured abortion.

Apostolic Exhortation Familiaris Consortio, 1981

✠ THE FAMILY, AS THE FUNDAMENTAL AND essential educating community, is the privileged means for transmitting the religious and cultural values which help the person to acquire his or her own identity. Founded on love and open to the gift of life, the family contains in itself the very future of society; its most special task is to contribute effectively to a future peace.

The Family Creates the Peace of the Human Family
World Day of Peace Message, January 1, 1994

✠ MARRIAGE AND THE FAMILY ARE INVARIABLY at the root of all the affairs of man and society. Although in itself it is, one might say, a most private concern, an affair of two persons, of husband and wife, and the smallest group, which they form together with their children, yet the fate of nations and continents, of humanity and the Church depends upon it.

Fruitful and Responsible Love, 1979

✠ [THE FAMILY] CONSTITUTES THE PRIMARY, fundamental and irreplaceable community.

The Family: Center of Love and Life
General Audience, December 31, 1978

MORALITY

THE HOLY FATHER SEES MODERN MAN'S MORAL conflicts as growing out of a misunderstanding of individualism, in which each person cares about nothing but his own advantage and counts himself free to pursue any behavior in his self-interest "as long as I don't hurt anyone else." The Pope finds such nihilistic individualism a totally inadequate basis for moral conduct.

Self-giving and self-surrender form the model for successful family life and describe the proper relationship between husbands and wives, children and parents, older and younger generations. This is also the model for justice and morality in the wider world. Yet justice is not a legal contract. While we must understand that others have the same rights as we do, such understanding is not sufficient. John Paul emphasizes that true justice lies in recognizing that others have not only rights, but also needs, and that all of God's children are deserving of having those needs fulfilled.

In relations between people, the ultimate lack of morality is to treat another as an object: to ask, "What can he or she do for me?" Selfishness and a misguided individualism are fatal to human dignity. The Lord Himself, who came "to serve rather than be served," offers the pattern of living that leads to Eternal Life.

MORALITY

✞ IT BECOMES NECESSARY, THEREFORE, ON THE part of all to recover an awareness of the primacy of moral values, which are the values of the human person as such. The great task that has to be faced today for the renewal of society is that of recapturing the ultimate meaning of life and its fundamental values.

Apostolic Exhortation Familiaris Consortio, *1981*

✞ EVERY AGE POSES NEW CHALLENGES AND NEW temptations for the People of God on their pilgrimage, and ours is no exception. We face a growing secularism that tries to exclude God and religious truth from human affairs. We face an insidious relativism that undermines the absolute truth of Christ and the truths of faith, and tempts believers to think of them as merely one set of beliefs or opinions among others. We face a materialistic consumerism that offers a whole series of pleasures that will never satisfy the human heart. All these attitudes can influence our sense of good and evil at the very moment when social and scientific progress requires strong ethical guidance. Once alienated from Christian faith and practice by these and other deceptions, people often commit themselves to passing fads, or to bizarre beliefs that are either shallow or fanatical.

Address at Monterey, California, September 17, 1987

✞ FORGIVENESS DEMONSTRATES THE PRESENCE in the world of the love which is more powerful than sin. Forgiveness is also the fundamental condition for reconciliation, not only in the relationship of God with man, but also in relationships between people. A world from which forgiveness was eliminated would be nothing but a world of cold and unfeeling justice in the name of which each person would claim his or her own rights vis-à-vis others; the various kinds of selfishness latent in man would transform life and human society into a system of oppression of the weak by the strong, or into an arena of permanent strife between one group and another.

Encyclical: Mercy of God (Dives in Misericordia), 1980

✠ WHY IS LIFE A GOOD? THIS QUESTION IS FOUND everywhere in the Bible, and from the very first pages it receives a powerful and amazing answer. The life which God gives man is quite different from the life of all other living creatures inasmuch as man, although formed from the dust of the earth (cf. Gn 2:7, 3:19; Jb 34:15; Pss 103:14, 104:29), is a manifestation of God in the world, a sign of His presence, a trace of His glory (cf. Gn 1:26–27; Ps 8:6).

Encyclical: The Gospel of Life (Evangelium Vitae), 1995

✠ LUST, AND IN PARTICULAR THE LUST of the body, is a specific threat to the structure of self-control and self-mastery, through which the human person is formed.

Blessed Are the Pure of Heart
General Audience, May 28, 1980

✠ TO CLAIM THE RIGHT TO ABORTION, INFANTICIDE and euthanasia, and to recognize that right in law, means to attribute to human freedom a perverse and evil significance: that of an absolute power over others and against others. This is the death of true freedom: "Truly, truly, I say to you, everyone who commits sin is a slave to sin" (Jn 8:34).

Encyclical: The Gospel of Life (Evangelium Vitae), 1995

✞ AMONG YOUR MANY ACTIVITIES AT THE SERVICE of life there is one which, especially at this juncture of history, deserves our firmest support: it is the continuing struggle against what the Second Vatican Council calls "the abominable crime" of abortion. Disregard for the sacred character of life in the womb weakens the very fabric of the acceptance of other practices that are against the fundamental rights of the individual.

Speech to Bishops at Los Angeles, September 1987

✞ MANY OF THE PROBLEMS [OF MODERN LIFE] are the result of a false notion of individual freedom at work in our culture, as if we could be free only when rejecting every objective norm of conduct, refusing to assume responsibility or even refusing to put curbs on instincts and passions! Instead, true freedom implies that we are capable of choosing a good without constraint. This is the truly human way of proceeding in the choices—big and small—which life puts before us.

Address at Columbia, South Carolina, September 11, 1987

✞ NOTHING "FROM OUTSIDE" MAKES MAN FILTHY, no "material" dirt makes man impure in the moral, that is, interior sense. No ablution, not even of a ritual nature, is capable in itself of producing moral purity. This has its exclusive source within man; it comes from the heart.

Blessed Are the Pure of Heart
General Audience, December 10, 1980

✞ IN THE MATERIALISTIC PERSPECTIVE INTER-personal relations are seriously impoverished. The first to be harmed are women, children, the sick or suffering, and the elderly. The criterion of personal dignity—which demands respect, generosity and service—is replaced by the criterion of efficiency, functionality and usefulness: others are considered not for what they "are," but for what they "have, do and produce." This is the supremacy of the strong over the weak.

Encyclical: The Gospel of Life (Evangelium Vitae), 1995

✠ FACED WITH PROBLEMS AND DISAPPOINTMENTS, many people will try to escape from their responsibility: escape in selfishness, escape in sexual pleasure, escape in drugs, escape in violence, escape in indifference and cynical attitudes. But today, I propose to you the option of love, which is the opposite of escape.

Address at Boston, October 1, 1979

✠ THE CHRISTIAN FAITH AND THE CHRISTIAN Church don't object to the depiction of evil in its various forms. Evil is a reality whose extent has been experienced and suffered in this century in the extreme by your country and mine. Without the reality of evil, the reality of good, redemption, mercy and salvation cannot be measured. This is not a license for evil, but rather an indication of its position.

Address at Munich, November 19, 1980

✠ THE CHURCH, HAVING BEFORE HER EYES THE picture of the generation to which we belong, shares the uneasiness of so many of the people of our time. Moreover, one cannot fail to be worried by the decline of many fundamental values, which constitute an unquestionable good not only for Christian morality but simply for human morality, for moral culture: these values include respect for human life from the moment of conception, respect for marriage in its indissoluble unity, and respect for the stability of the family.

Encyclical: Mercy of God (Dives in Misericordia), 1980

✠ MERCY IN ITSELF, AS A PERFECTION OF THE
infinite God, is also infinite. Also infinite therefore and in-
exhaustible is the Father's readiness to receive the prodigal
children who return to His home. Infinite are the readiness and
power of forgiveness which flow continually from the marvelous
value of the sacrifice of the Son. No human sin can prevail over
this power or even limit it.

Encyclical: Mercy of God
(Dives in Misericordia), 1980

✠ ON A MORE GENERAL LEVEL, THERE EXISTS
in contemporary culture a certain Promethean attitude
which leads people to think that they can control life and
death by taking the decisions about them into their own hands.
What really happens in this case is that the individual is overcome and crushed by a death deprived of any prospect of meaning or hope. We see a tragic expression of all this in the spread of
euthanasia—disguised and surreptitious or practiced openly and
even legally.

Encyclical: The Gospel of Life
(Evangelium Vitae), 1995

✠ ONE OF THE KEY PASTORAL PROBLEMS FACING
us is the widespread misunderstanding of the role of conscience, whereby individual conscience and experience
are exalted above or against Church teaching. The young women
and men of America, and indeed of the whole Western world,
who are often victims of educational theories which propose that
they "create" their own values and that "feeling good about themselves" is a primary guiding moral principle, are asking to be led
out of this moral confusion.

Ad Limina *Address to Bishops from New England,*
September 21, 1993

✠ IN A TECHNOLOGICAL CULTURE IN WHICH people are used to dominating matter, discovering its laws and mechanisms in order to transform it according to their wishes, the danger arises of also wanting to manipulate conscience and its demands. In a culture which holds that no universally valid truths are possible, nothing is absolute. Therefore, in the end—they say—objective goodness and evil no longer really matter. Good comes to mean what is pleasing or useful at a particular moment. Evil means what contradicts our subjective wishes. Each person can build a private system of values.

Prayer Vigil at World Youth Day, August 26, 1993

✠ A TEMPERATE MAN IS ONE WHO DOES NOT abuse food, drink, pleasures; who does not drink alcoholic beverages to excess; who does not deprive himself of consciousness by using drugs or narcotics. We can imagine within us a "lower self" and a "higher self." In our "lower self" our "body" is expressed with its needs, its desires, its passions of sensible nature. The virtue of temperance guarantees every man the control of the "lower self" by the "higher self." Is it a question, in this case, of a humiliation, a disability, for our body? On the contrary! This control gives it new value, exalts it.

Vatican Address, November 22, 1978

✠ THE GREATEST OBSTACLE TO MAN'S JOURNEY toward God is sin, perseverance in sin and, finally, denial of God—the deliberate blotting out of God from the world of human thought, the detachment from Him of the whole of man's earthly activity, the rejection of God by man.

The Message of Fatima, May 13, 1982

✞ THE MAN OF TODAY SEEMS EVER TO BE UNDER threat from what he produces, that is to say, from the result of the work of his hands and, even more so, the work of his intellect and the tendencies of his will. All too soon, and often in an unforeseeable way, what this manifold activity of man yields is not only subjected to "alienation," in the sense that it is simply taken away from the person who produces it, but rather it turns against man himself, at least in part, through the indirect consequences of its effects returning on himself. It is or can be directed against him. This seems to make up the main chapter of the drama of present-day human existence in its broadest and universal dimension.

Encyclical: The Redeemer of Man (Redemptor Hominis), 1979

PEACE

JOHN PAUL'S STAND IN FAVOR OF PEACE TAKES NO political position. He has spoken out against the Shining Path guerrillas in South America as forcefully as he has against the Iraqi invasion of Kuwait and the American-led war on Iraq. And he has carried his message even to countries actually at war, as he did in Britain during the Falkland Islands war in 1983.

For John Paul one of the tragedies of war-making is the effect on the poor. He has observed that the vast arms arsenals of the world are bought at the cost of depriving the poor of the necessities of life, most evidently in Third World countries, but even in the industrialized West. And extreme poverty itself, in the Holy Father's view, is a grave threat to peace.

The Pope also links peace with religious liberty. He believes that true religious feeling promotes true peace, and that if public authorities ensure religious liberty, they are also furthering the cause of peace. Nor is he unaware that governments are capable of preaching peace and making war simultaneously. Peace, he reminds us, is not a slogan to be used to reassure or to deceive.

John Paul is not a pacifist, and he has said so. He has never denied the necessity to wage war against aggression. But he constantly appeals to warring parties to come together to discuss peace.

The guarantor of peace, in the Holy Father's view, is moral principle, and whatever the social causes of war, personal moral responsibility is central. Without it, no peace can last.

PEACE

✠ PEACE IS NOT A UTOPIA, NOR AN INACCESSIBLE
ideal, nor an unrealizable dream. War is not an inevitable
calamity. Peace is possible.

Negotiation: The Only Realistic Solution to the
Continuing Threat of War, June 1982

✠ THE CATHOLIC CHURCH IN EVERY PLACE ON
earth proclaims a message of peace, prays for peace, edu-
cates for peace. This purpose is also shared by the representatives and followers of other churches and communities and
of other religions of the world, and they have pledged themselves
to it. In union with efforts by all people of good will, this work is
certainly bearing fruit. Nevertheless, we are continually troubled
by the armed conflicts that break out from time to time.

Speech at the United Nations, October 2, 1979

✠ WAR IS THE WORK OF MAN. WAR IS THE
destruction of human life. War is death. Nowhere do
these truths impose themselves upon us more forcefully
than in this city of Hiroshima, at this Peace Memorial.

Address at the Peace Memorial, Hiroshima, February 25, 1981

✠ IN CURRENT CONDITIONS, "DETERRENCE" BASED
on balance, certainly not as an end in itself but as a step
on the way toward a progressive disarmament, may still
be judged morally acceptable. Nonetheless, in order to ensure
peace, it is indispensable not to be satisfied with this minimum
which is always susceptible to the real danger of explosion.

Negotiation: The Only Realistic Solution to the
Continuing Threat of War, June 1982

✠ IN FACT, NUCLEAR WEAPONS ARE NOT THE ONLY means of war and destruction. The production and sale of conventional weapons throughout the world is a truly alarming and evidently growing phenomenon. No negotiations about armaments would be complete if they were to ignore the fact that 80 percent of the expenditures for weapons are devoted to conventional arms. Moreover, the traffic in these weapons seems to be developing at an increasing rate and seems to be directed most of all toward developing countries. Every step taken to limit this production and traffic and to bring them under an ever more effective control will be an important contribution to the cause of peace.

Negotiation: The Only Realistic Solution to the Continuing Threat of War, June 1982

✠ IN OUR MODERN WORLD, TO REFUSE PEACE means not only to provoke the sufferings and the loss that—today more than ever—war, even a limited one, implies; it could also involve the total destruction of entire regions, not to mention the threat of possible or probable catastrophes in ever vaster and possibly even universal proportions.

Negotiation: The Only Realistic Solution to the Continuing Threat of War, June 1982

✠ THE ANCIENTS SAID: "SI VIS PAREM, PARA bellum" [If you want peace, prepare for war]. But can our age still really believe that the breathtaking spiral of armaments is at the service of world peace? In alleging the threat of a potential enemy, is it not really rather the intention to keep for oneself a means of threat, in order to get the upper hand with the aid of one's own arsenal of destruction? Here too it is the human dimension of peace that tends to vanish in favor of ever new possible forms of imperialism.

Speech at the United Nations, October 2, 1979

✠ THE SECOND HALF OF OUR CENTURY, IN ITS TURN, brings with it—as though in proportion to the mistakes and transgressions of our contemporary civilization—such a horrible threat of nuclear war that we cannot think of this period except in terms of an incomparable accumulation of sufferings, even to the possible self-destruction of humanity.

Apostolic Letter on the Christian Meaning of Holy Suffering, 1984

✠ WHERE THERE IS NO JUSTICE — WHO DOES NOT know it—there cannot be peace, because injustice is already a disorder and the word of the prophet remains true: "opus justitia pax" ("the work of justice is peace"; Is 32:17). Likewise, where there is no respect for human rights—I speak of inalienable rights inherent in the person as person—there cannot be peace, because every violation of personal dignity favors rancor and the spirit of vendetta.

Christmas Address, December 22, 1978

✠ THE EMBARGO IN PARTICULAR, CLEARLY DEFINED by law, is an instrument which needs to be used with great discernment, and it must be subjected to strict legal and ethical criteria. It is a means of exerting pressure on governments which have violated the international code of good conduct and of causing them to reconsider their choices. But in a sense it is also an act of force and, as certain cases of the present moment demonstrate, it inflicts grave hardships upon the people of the countries at which it is aimed. I often receive appeals for help from individuals suffering from confinement and extreme poverty. Here I would like to remind you who are diplomats that, before imposing such measures, it is always imperative to foresee the humanitarian consequences of sanctions, without failing to respect the just proportion that such measures should have in relation to the very evil which they are meant to remedy.

Averting Civilization's Ruin
Address to Diplomatic Corps, January 19, 1995

✠ WE ALL KNOW WELL THAT THE AREAS OF MISERY
and hunger on our globe could have been made fertile in
a short time, if the gigantic investments for armaments at
the service of war and destruction had been changed into investments for food at the service of life.

Encyclical: The Redeemer of Man (Redemptor Hominis), 1979

✠ THE DUTY OF PEACE FALLS ESPECIALLY UPON
the leaders of the world. It is up to the representatives of
governments and peoples to work to free humanity not
only from wars and conflicts but from the fear that is generated by
ever more sophisticated and deadly weapons. Peace is not only
the absence of war; it also involves reciprocal trust between nations—a trust that is manifested and proved through constructive
negotiations that aim at ending the arms race, and at liberating
immense resources that can be used to alleviate misery and feed
millions of hungry human beings.

At Meeting with President Reagan, June 7, 1982

✠ TO REMEMBER HIROSHIMA IS TO COMMIT
oneself to peace. To remember what the people of this city
suffered is to renew our faith in man, in his capacity to do
what is good, in his freedom to choose what is right, in his determination to turn disaster into a new beginning. In the face of the
man-made calamity that every war is, one must affirm and reaffirm again and again that the waging of war is not inevitable or
unchangeable. Humanity is not destined to self-destruction.

Address at the Peace Memorial, Hiroshima, February 25, 1981

PRAYER

RAYER IS A CONVERSATION WITH GOD, AND GOD'S invitation to pray, to converse with Him, is proof of the high esteem in which He holds human beings. John Paul emphasizes strongly the importance of individual dignity in this matter—prayer is an individual speaking directly to God.

In the family, prayer becomes an expression of the family's union with Christ. All the important moments of family life—births and deaths, wedding anniversaries and birthdays, homecomings and departures, important decisions and family crises—should be the occasion for prayer. Parents must set an example by praying themselves, and praying with their children.

This private or familial prayer should be the prelude to the liturgical prayer of the Church, and especially to participation in the celebration of the Mass. By observing the liturgical year and its holidays, the family can help to integrate private prayer into the public prayer of the Church. Private prayer is sustained by the ministry of the Church, and especially by the sacraments of penance and Holy Eucharist.

Prayer

✝ O Virgin Mother,
   guide and sustain us
   so that we might always live
   as true sons and daughters
   of the Church of your Son.
   Enable us to do our part
   in helping to establish on earth
   the civilization of truth and love,
   as God wills it,
   for His glory.
   Amen.

Apostolic Exhortation, Christifideles Laici, 1988, *December 30, 1988*

✝ PRAYER CALLS US TO EXAMINE OUR CONSCIENCES on all the issues that affect humanity. It calls us to ponder our personal and collective responsibility before the judgment of God and in the light of human solidarity. Hence prayer is able to transform the world. Everything is new with prayer, both for individuals and for communities. New goals and new ideals emerge. Christian dignity and action are reaffirmed. The commitments of our Baptism, Confirmation and Holy Orders take on new urgency. The horizons of conjugal love and of the mission of the family are vastly extended in prayer.

Speech at Atlanta, Georgia, June 10, 1988

✝ IF YOU REALLY WISH TO FOLLOW CHRIST, IF YOU want your love for Him to grow and last, then you must be faithful to prayer. It is the key to the vitality of your life in Christ. Without prayer, your faith and love will die. If you are constant in daily prayer and in the Sunday celebration of Mass, your love for Jesus will increase. And your heart will know deep joy and peace.

Speech at New Orleans, September 12, 1987

✠ WHEN IT IS DIFFICULT THEREFORE TO PRAY, THE most important thing is not to stop praying, not to give up the effort. At these times, turn to the Bible and go to the Church's liturgy. Meditate on the life and teachings of Jesus as recorded in the Gospels. Ponder the wisdom and counsel of the Apostles and the challenging messages of the Prophets. Try to make your own the beautiful prayers of the psalms. You will find in the inspired word of God the spiritual food you need. Above all, your soul will be refreshed when you take part wholeheartedly with the community in the celebration of the Eucharist, the Church's greatest prayer.

Speech at New Orleans, September 12, 1987

✠ THROUGH THE PRAYER OF CHRIST TO WHICH WE give voice, our day is sanctified, our activities transformed, our actions made holy. We pray the same psalms that Jesus prayed and come into personal contact with Him—the person to whom all Scripture points, the goal to which all history is directed.

Speech at St. Patrick's Cathedral, New York City, October 3, 1979

✠ IT IS SIGNIFICANT THAT PRECISELY IN AND through prayer man comes to discover in a very simple and yet profound way his own unique subjectivity: in prayer the human "I" more easily perceives the depth of what it means to be a person.

Letter to Families for the International Year of the Family, February 22, 1994

✠ PRAYER INCREASES THE STRENGTH AND SPIRITUAL
unity of the family, helping the family to partake of God's
own "strength."

Letter to Families for the International Year of the Family,
February 22, 1994

✠ THERE ARE SEVERAL DEFINITIONS OF PRAYER.
But it is most often called a talk, a conversation, a collo-
quy with God. Conversing with someone, not only do we
speak but we also listen. Prayer, therefore, is also listening. It consists of listening to hear the interior voice of grace. Listening to
hear the call. And then, as you ask me how the Pope prays, I answer you: like every Christian—he speaks and he listens. Sometimes, he prays without words, and then he listens all the more.
The most important thing is precisely what he "hears." And he
also tries to unite prayer with his obligations, his activities, his
work, and to unite his work with prayer. In this way, day after day,
he tries to carry out his "service," his "ministry," which comes to
him from the will of Christ and from the living tradition of the
Church.

Address to the Institut Catholique, Paris,
June 1, 1980

✠ PRAYER CAN TRULY CHANGE YOUR LIFE. FOR IT
turns your attention away from yourself and directs your
mind and your heart toward the Lord. If we look only at
ourselves, with our own limitations and sins, we quickly give way
to sadness and discouragement. But if we keep our eyes fixed on
the Lord, then our hearts are filled with hope, our minds are
washed in the light of truth, and we come to know the fullness of
the Gospel with all its promise and life.

Address to Youth at New Orleans,
September 12, 1987

✠ ONLY A WORSHIPPING AND PRAYING CHURCH can show herself sufficiently sensitive to the needs of the sick, the suffering, the lonely—especially in the great urban centers—and the poor everywhere. The Church as a community of service has first to feel the weight of the burden carried by so many individuals and families, and then strive to help alleviate these burdens. The discipleship that the Church discovers in prayer she expresses in deep interest for Christ's brethren in the modern world and for their many different needs. Her concern, manifested in various ways, embraces—among others—the areas of housing, education, health care, unemployment, the administration of justice, the special needs of the aged and the handicapped. In prayer, the Church is confirmed in her solidarity with the weak who are oppressed, the vulnerable who are manipulated, the children who are exploited, and everyone who is in any way discriminated against.

Ad Limina *Address to U.S. Bishops, December 3, 1983*

✠ THE UNIVERSAL CHURCH OF CHRIST, AND therefore each particular Church, exists in order to pray. In prayer the human person expresses his or her nature; the community expresses its vocation; the Church reaches out to God. In prayer the Church attains fellowship with the Father and with His Son, Jesus Christ (see 1 Jn 1:3). In prayer the Church expresses her Trinitarian life, because she directs herself to the Father, undergoes the action of the Holy Spirit and lives fully her relationship with Christ. Indeed, she experiences herself as the Body of Christ, and the mystical Christ.

Address to Bishops at Atlanta, June 10, 1988

✠ IT SHOULD NEVER BE FORGOTTEN THAT PRAYER constitutes an essential part of Christian life, understood in its fullness and centrality. Indeed, prayer is an important part of our very humanity: it is "the first expression of man's inner truth, the first condition for authentic freedom of spirit."

Apostolic Exhortation Familiaris Consortio, 1981

✠ FAMILY PRAYER HAS FOR ITS VERY OWN OBJECT family life itself, which in all its varying circumstances is seen as a call from God and lived as a filial response to His call. Joys and sorrows, hopes and disappointments, births and birthday celebrations, wedding anniversaries of the parents, departures, separations and homecomings, important and far-reaching decisions, the death of those who are dear, etc.—all of these mark God's loving intervention in the family's history. They should be seen as suitable moments for thanksgiving, for petition, for trusting abandonment of the family into the hands of their common Father in heaven.

Apostolic Exhortation Familiaris Consortio, 1981

✠ THE TRUTH OF PRAYER IS BOTH THE CAUSE and the effect of a lifestyle which is placed in the light of the Gospel.

World Mission Day Message, October 18, 1981

✠ IN LIGHT OF THIS DIFFICULTY WE MUST DEMON-strate incessantly that Christian prayer is inseparable from our faith in God, Father, Son and Holy Spirit, from our faith in His love and His redeeming power, which is at work in the world. Therefore, prayer is worthwhile above all for us: Lord, "increase our faith" (Lk 17:6). It has as its goal our conversion, that is, as St. Cyprian explained, interior and exterior openness, the will to open oneself to the transforming action of grace.

World Mission Day Message, October 18, 1981

✠ THE ROSARY IS MY FAVORITE PRAYER. A MAR-
velous prayer! Marvelous in its simplicity and in its depth.

In the prayer we repeat many times the words that the
Virgin Mary heard from the Archangel, and from her kinswoman
Elizabeth.

Vatican Address, October 26, 1978

AN EVER INCREASING NUMBER OF SCIENTISTS are becoming aware of their human responsibility and are convinced that there cannot be science without conscience. This fundamental thought is a positive and encouraging gain of our own time, which is better able to measure the limits of scientism, which one should take good care not to identify with science itself.

Address at the University of Fribourg, Switzerland,
June 13, 1984

THE VARIOUS TECHNIQUES OF ARTIFICIAL reproduction, which would seem to be at the service of life and which are frequently used with this intention, actually open the door to new threats against life. The number of embryos produced is often greater than that needed for implantation in the woman's womb, and these so-called spare embryos are then destroyed or used for research which, under the pretext of scientific or medical progress, in fact reduces human life to the level of simple "biological material" to be freely disposed of.

Encyclical: The Gospel of Life (Evangelium Vitae), 1995

WE MUST CONVINCE OURSELVES OF THE priority of ethics over technology, of the primacy of person over things, of the superiority of spirit over matter.

The Freedom of Conscience and Religions, September 1, 1980

[TECHNOLOGY] FACILITATES [MAN'S] WORK, perfects, accelerates and augments it. It leads to an increase in the quantity of things produced by work, and in many cases improves their quality. However, it is also a fact that in some instances technology can cease to be man's ally and become almost his enemy, as when the mechanization of work

PROGRESS AND THE MODERN WORLD

THE SEARCH FOR SCIENTIFIC TRUTH IS EXTREMELY important to this highly intellectual and scientifically minded Pope. To the Holy Father, applying reason to nature is a worthy pursuit, and the products of such work are a positive good. Science has great potential as a unifying force, and thus creates no conflict with religion. In fact, scientific progress serves spiritual progress, because through science and technology we free ourselves to pursue good works and service to others.

John Paul has urged theologians to eliminate scientific ignorance by entering into a meaningful dialogue with scientists. When he remarked in 1979 that "Galileo suffered greatly at the hands of churchmen," he was referring to an ignorance of science. He urges theologians and scientists alike to "be aware of our own competencies" and always to be faithful to the truth, because "the truth shall make you free."

Furthermore, scientists, who study the body merely as a machine, achieve an impressive but nevertheless limited truth and understanding: the human body has a spiritual component, which cannot be ignored or denied.

John Paul calls upon scientists to take responsibility for their research, particularly in the areas of genetics and nuclear science, the first because it may allow a person to be converted into a means rather than respected as an individual, and the second because it can, in certain applications, threaten continued life on earth.

Far from opposing development, John Paul sees underdevelopment as a source of injustice, poverty, and war. When he criticizes the material preoccupations of rich countries, it is not because he is interested in slowing progress but because he believes that where the search for increasing material wealth dominates, there can be no real progress. True progress requires not only the satisfaction of material needs but the achievement of spiritual fulfillment as well.

✝ THE DOMINION GRANTED TO MAN BY THE Creator is not an absolute power, nor can one speak of a freedom to "use and misuse," or to dispose of things as one pleases. The limitation imposed from the beginning by the Creator Himself and expressed symbolically by the prohibition not to "eat of the fruit of the tree" (cf. Gn 2:16–17) shows clearly enough that, when it comes to the natural world, we are subject not only to biological laws but also to moral ones, which cannot be violated with impunity.

Encyclical: On Social Concerns
(Sollicitudo Rei Socialis), 1987

✝ ANY PROGRESS WHICH WOULD SECURE THE betterment of a select few at the expense of the great human family would be an erroneous and distorted progress. It would be an outrage against the demands of justice and an affront to the dignity of every human being.

Building Up the Body of Christ
Pastoral Visit to the United States, 1987

✝ IT IS THE ECOLOGICAL QUESTION — RANGING from the preservation of the natural habitats of the different species of animals and of other forms of life to human ecology properly speaking—which finds in the Bible clear and strong ethical direction leading to a solution which respects great good of life, of every life.

Encyclical: The Gospel of Life
(Evangelium Vitae), 1995

"supplants" him, taking away all personal satisfaction and the incentive to creativity and responsibility.

Encyclical: On Human Work (Laborem Exercens), 1981

✠ SURELY WE MUST BE GRATEFUL FOR THE NEW technology which enables us to store information in vast man-made artificial memories, thus providing wide and instant access to the knowledge which is our human heritage, to the Church's teaching and tradition, the words of Sacred Scripture, the counsels of the great masters of spirituality, the history and traditions of the local churches, of religious orders and lay institutes, and to the ideas and experiences of initiators and innovators whose insights bear constant witness to the faithful presence in our midst of a loving Father who brings out of His treasure house new things and old.

The Church Must Learn to Cope with the
Computer Culture Statement Issued on World
Communication Day, May 27, 1989

✠ SCIENCE IN THE FIELD OF BIOPHYSIOLOGY AND biomedicine has made great progress. However, this science deals with man under a determined "aspect" and so is practical rather than global. We know well the functions connected with the masculinity and femininity of the human person, but this science does not yet develop the awareness of the body as a sign of the person, as a manifestation of the spirit.

Blessed Are the Pure of Heart
General Audience, April 8, 1981

✠ OUR PERIOD AND THE PERIODS THAT PRECEDED IT too easily believed that scientific and technological conquests would be the equivalent, or at least the guarantee, of human progress, which would bring about freedom and happiness. In our own day, many scholars as well as an increasing number of our contemporaries are realizing that the rash transformation of the world risks jeopardizing in a grave way the complex and delicate equilibrium that exists in nature.

Address at the University of Fribourg, Switzerland, June 13, 1984

✠ WITH THE ADVENT OF COMPUTER TELE-communications and what are known as computer participation systems, the Church is offered further means for fulfilling her mission. Methods of facilitating communication and dialogue among her own members can strengthen the bonds of unity between them. Immediate access to information makes it possible for her to deepen her dialogue with the contemporary world.

The Church Must Learn to Cope with the Computer Culture
Statement Issued on World Communication Day, May 27, 1989

✠ TODAY WE ARE CONCERNED TO SEE THE DESERT expanding to lands which only yesterday were prosperous and fertile. We cannot forget that in many cases man himself has been the cause of the barrenness of lands which have become desert, just as he has caused the pollution of formerly clean waters. When people do not respect the goods of the earth, when they abuse them, they act unjustly, even criminally, because for many of their brothers and sisters their actions result in poverty and death.

The World's Expanding Deserts
Lenten Message, January 7, 1993

✠ MANY TIMES IN RECENT YEARS, THE CHURCH has addressed issues related to the advances in biomedical technology. She does so not in order to discourage scientific progress or to judge harshly those who seek to extend the frontiers of human knowledge and skill, but in order to affirm the moral truths which must guide the application of this knowledge and skill. Ultimately, the purpose of the Church's teaching in this field is to defend the innate dignity and fundamental rights of the human person. In this regard the Church cannot fail to emphasize the need to safeguard the life and integrity of the human embryo and fetus.

Address at Phoenix, September 14, 1987

✠ ALL OF US, IN SOME WAY, EXPERIENCE SORROW and suffering in our lives. No amount of economic, scientific or social progress can eradicate our vulnerability to sin and to death.

Homily at Mass in Los Angeles Coliseum, September 15, 1987

✠ THE PENCHANT FOR EMPIRICAL OBSERVATION, the procedures of scientific objectification, technological progress and certain forms of liberalism have led to these two terms being set in opposition, as if a dialectic, if not an absolute conflict, between freedom and nature were characteristic of the structure of human history. At other periods, it seemed that "nature" subjected man totally to its own dynamics and even its own unbreakable laws. Today too, the situation of the world of the senses within space and time, physicochemical constants, bodily processes, psychological impulses and forms of social conditioning seem to many people the only really decisive factors of human reality. In this context even moral facts, despite their specificity, are frequently treated as if they were statistically verifiable data, patterns of behavior which can be subject to observation or explained exclusively in categories of psychosocial processes.

Encyclical: The Splendor of Truth (Veritatis Splendor), 1993

✝ OUR CIVILIZATION, ESPECIALLY IN THE WEST—
connected as it is with the development of science and
technique—glimpses the need of the intellectual and
physical effort. It does not, on the other hand, sufficiently consider the importance of the effort necessary to recover and promote moral values, which constitute the most authentic inner life
of man. And it pays for it with that sense of emptiness and confusion which the young feel especially, sometimes even dramati-
cally.

Address to Young People, 1979

✝ THE PROSPECT OF GROWING ECONOMIC
progress, and the chance of obtaining a greater share of
the goods that modern society has to offer, will appear to
you as an opportunity to achieve greater freedom. The more
you possess—you may be tempted to think—the more you will
feel liberated from every type of confinement. In order to make
more money and to possess more, in order to eliminate effort
and worry, you may be tempted to take moral shortcuts where
honesty, truth and work are concerned. The progress of science
and technology seems inevitable and you may be enticed to
look toward the technological society for the answers to all your
problems.

Address at Dublin, September 29, 1979

✝ SCIENTIFIC AND TECHNOLOGICAL PROGRESS,
which contemporary man is continually expanding in his
dominion over nature, not only offers the hope of creating
new and better humanity, but also causes ever greater anxiety regarding the future. Some ask themselves if it is a good thing to be
alive or if it would be better never to have been born; they doubt
therefore if it is right to bring others into life when perhaps they
will curse their existence in a cruel world with unforeseeable ter-

rors. Others consider themselves to be the only ones for whom the advantages of technology are intended, and they exclude others by imposing on them contraceptives or even worse means. Still others, imprisoned in a consumer mentality and solely concerned with bringing about a continual growth of material goods, finish by ceasing to understand, and thus by refusing, the spiritual riches of a new human life. The ultimate reason for these mentalities is the absence in people's hearts of God, whose love alone is stronger than all the world's fears and can conquer them.

Apostolic Exhortation Familiaris Consortio, 1981

RICH AND POOR

Perhaps John Paul's most memorable words on the responsibility of the rich to the poor were spoken at Yankee Stadium in 1979, when he urged rich countries such as the United States to treat the poor "like guests at your family table," not leaving them merely "the crumbs of the feast," but having them take part in the substance of the meal. Equitable distribution of the world's material bounty has been his constant plea and his consistent concern.

John Paul ties spiritual freedom and freedom from material want closely together. Where extreme poverty dominates, spiritual values collapse and violence flourishes. In this sense, both material and spiritual goods are unequally distributed in the world, and this imbalance must be adjusted.

John Paul is impatient with those who passively notice and pity the poor. Love for the poor, in his view, has to result in deeds. The poor cannot be ignored with the justification that there is a better world awaiting them. Individuals with great riches must share them; families with two incomes must share with those who have none; nations blessed with ample material wealth must share it with those that have little. The Holy Father urges that all have "a special preference" for the poor and the hungry, not just a passive concern.

The Pope can be very specific about what a "special preference" for the poor means, particularly so regarding the redistribution of wealth. He has not hesitated to embrace the poor, even the revolutionary poor, in their fight against the evil of poverty.

RICH AND POOR

✠ IF YOU ONLY WANT TO HAVE MORE AND MORE,
if your idol is profit and pleasure, remember that man's
value is not measured by what he has, but by what he is.
So let him who has accumulated a great deal, and who thinks that
everything is summed up in this, remember that he may be worth
far less (within himself and in the eyes of God) than any of those
poor and unknown persons.

Address to Indians of Amazonia, June 30, 1980

✠ ONE OF THE GREATEST INJUSTICES IN THE CON-
temporary world consists precisely in this: that the ones
who possess much are relatively few and those who possess almost nothing are many. It is the injustice of the poor distribution of the goods and services originally intended for all.

Encyclical: On Social Concerns (Sollicitudo Rei Socialis), 1987

✠ SURMOUNTING EVERY TYPE OF IMPERIALISM
and determination to preserve their own hegemony, the
stronger and richer nations must have a sense of moral responsibility for the other nations, so that a real international system may be established which will rest on the foundation of the
equality of all peoples and on the necessary respect for their legitimate differences. The economically weaker countries, or those
still at subsistence level, must be enabled, with the assistance of
other peoples and of the international community, to make a contribution of their own to the common good with their treasures of
humanity and culture, which otherwise would be lost forever.

Encyclical: On Social Concerns (Sollicitudo Rei Socialis), 1987

✠ THE PERSON WHO, LIKE THE RICH LANDOWNER in the Gospel parable, thinks that he can make his life secure by the possession of material goods alone is deluding himself. Life is slipping away from him, and very soon he will find himself bereft of it without ever having appreciated its real meaning: "Fool! This night your soul is required of you; and the things you have prepared, whose will they be?" (Lk 12:20).

Encyclical: The Gospel of Life (Evangelium Vitae), 1995

✠ A DISCONCERTING CONCLUSION ABOUT THE most recent period should serve to enlighten us: side-by-side with the miseries of underdevelopment, themselves unacceptable, we find ourselves up against a form of superdevelopment, equally inadmissible, because like the former it is contrary to what is good and to true happiness. This superdevelopment, which consists in an excessive availability of every kind of material goods for the benefit of certain social groups, easily makes people slaves of "possession" and of immediate gratification, with no other horizon than the multiplication or continual replacement of the things already owned with others still better. This is the so-called civilization of "consumption" or "consumerism," which involves so much "throwing away" and "waste."

Encyclical: On Social Concerns (Sollicitudo Rei Socialis), 1987

✠ WHEN THE WEST GIVES THE IMPRESSION OF abandoning itself to forms of growing and selfish isolation, and the East in its turn seems to ignore for questionable reasons its duty to cooperate in the task of alleviating human misery, then we are up against not only a betrayal of humanity's legitimate expectations—a betrayal that is a harbinger of unforeseeable consequences—but also a real desertion of a moral obligation.

Encyclical: On Social Concerns (Sollicitudo Rei Socialis), 1987

✠ THE HOMELESS MAKE UP A GROUP THAT IS still poorer than the poor; all of us need to help them. We are convinced that a house is much more than a simple roof over one's head. The place where a person creates and lives out his or her life also serves to found, in some way, that person's deepest identity and his or her relations with others.

Negotiation: The Only Realistic Solution to the
Continuing Threat of War, June 1982

✠ SOCIAL THINKING AND SOCIAL PRACTICE inspired by the Gospel must always be marked by a special sensitivity toward those who are most in distress, those who are extremely poor, those suffering from all the physical, mental and moral ills that afflict humanity, including hunger, neglect, unemployment and despair.

Homily at Yankee Stadium, New York, October 2, 1979

✠ WITHOUT GOING INTO AN ANALYSIS OF FIGURES and statistics, it is sufficient to face squarely the reality of an innumerable multitude of people—children, adults and the elderly—in other words, real and unique human persons, who are suffering under the intolerable burden of poverty.

Encyclical: On Social Concerns (Sollicitudo Rei Socialis), 1987

✠ THE POOR OF THE UNITED STATES AND OF THE world are your brothers and sisters in Christ. You must never be content to leave them just the crumbs from the feast. You must take of your substance, and not just of your abundance, in order to help them. And you must treat them like guests at your family table.

Homily at Yankee Stadium, New York, October 2, 1979

✝ RECALL THE TIME WHEN JESUS SAW THE HUNGRY crowd gathered on the hillside. What was His response? He did not content Himself with expressing His compassion. He gave His disciples the command, "Give them something to eat yourselves" (Mt 14:16). Did He not intend those same words for us today, for us who live at the closing of the twentieth century, for us who have the means available to feed the hungry of the world?

Address at Des Moines, Iowa, October 4, 1979

✝ IN THE LIGHT OF CHRIST'S WORDS, THIS POOR South will judge the rich North. And the poor people and poor nations—poor in different ways, not only lacking food, but also deprived of freedom and other human rights—will judge those people who take these goods away from them, amassing to themselves the imperialistic monopoly of economic and political supremacy at the expense of others.

Homily at Edmonton, Alberta, September 17, 1984

✝ THE CHURCH ALL OVER THE WORLD WISHES TO be the Church of the poor . . . that is, she wishes to extract all the truth contained in the Beatitudes of Christ and especially in this first one: "Blessed are the poor in spirit. . . ." She wishes to teach this truth and to put it into practice, just as Jesus came to do and to teach.

Address to the Indians of Amazonia, June 30, 1980

✝ EVEN IN THIS WEALTHY NATION, COMMITTED by its founding fathers to the dignity and equality of all persons, the black community suffers a disproportionate share of economic deprivation. Far too many of our young people receive less than an equal opportunity for a quality education and for gainful employment. The Church must continue to join her effort with the efforts of others who are working to correct all imbalances and disorders of a social nature. Indeed, the Church can never remain silent in the face of injustice wherever it is clearly present.

Address at New Orleans, September 12, 1987

✟ THE NUMBER OF PEOPLE LIVING IN EXTREME poverty is enormous. I am thinking, for example, of the tragic situations in certain countries of Africa, Asia and Latin America. There exist vast groups, often whole sectors of the population, which find themselves on the margins of civil life within their own countries. Among them is a growing number of children who in order to survive can rely on nobody except themselves. Such a situation is not only an affront to human dignity but also represents a clear threat to peace. A state, whatever its political organization or economic system, remains fragile and unstable if it does not give constant attention to its weakest members and if it fails to do everything possible to ensure that at least their primary needs are satisfied.

The Links Between Poverty and Peace
1993 World Day of Peace Message, December 11, 1992

✟ IN THE INTEREST OF THE INDIVIDUAL — AND thus of peace — it is urgently necessary to introduce into the mechanisms of the economy the necessary correctives which will enable the mechanisms to ensure a more just and equitable distribution of good. By itself the rules of the market are not sufficient to accomplish this; society must accept its own responsibilities. It must do so by increasing its efforts, which are often already considerable, to eliminate the causes of poverty and their tragic consequences. No country by itself can succeed in such an undertaking. For this very reason it is necessary to work together, with that solidarity demanded by a world which has become ever more interdependent. To allow situations of extreme poverty to persist is to create social conditions ever more exposed to the threat of violence and conflict.

The Links Between Poverty and Peace
1993 World Day of Peace Message, December 11, 1992

✝ DEVELOPMENT CANNOT CONSIST ONLY IN THE use, dominion over, and indiscriminate possession of created things and the products of human industry, but rather in subordinating the possessions, dominion and the use to man's divine likeness and to his vocation to immortality.

Encyclical: On Social Concerns (Sollicitudo Rei Socialis), 1987

✝ IN THE FINAL ANALYSIS, HOWEVER, WE MUST realize that social injustice and unjust social structures exist only because individuals and groups of individuals deliberately maintain or tolerate them. It is these personal choices, operating through structures, that breed and propagate situations of poverty, oppression and misery. For this reason, overcoming "social" sin and reforming the social order itself must begin with the conversion of our hearts. As the American bishops have said: "The Gospel confers on each Christian the vocation to love God and neighbor in ways that bear fruit in the life of society. That vocation consists above all in a change of heart: a conversion expressed in praise of God and in concrete deeds of justice and service."

Economic Justice for All: Catholic Social Teaching
and the U.S. Economy
Address to Catholic Charities, California, September 19, 1987

SUFFERING, DYING, AND DEATH

CHRIST'S DEATH ON THE CROSS UNITES PHYSICAL and spiritual suffering: He took upon Himself the moral evil of sin, and suffered for that.

John Paul has himself suffered considerable physical pain, both in his younger years and more recently. The wound he received in the attempt on his life is well known; a recent stay in a hospital after a fall was terribly painful for him. He has an almost mystical sense of himself as suffering for all mankind. From his hospital bed in May 1994, he referred to his present physical pain and to the attempt on his life more than a decade before as evidence that the Pope must suffer, in a sense taking on the pain that others suffer.

John Paul emphasizes that in the face of the suffering of others, compassion and sympathy, however heartfelt, are not enough.

Action to relieve suffering is the only moral course, an obligation that cannot be evaded. On the other hand, suffering can transform us, teach us compassion, and so draw us closer to Christ. Through suffering we—like Him—take part in saving the world. Thus "in our own sufferings we find inner peace, even spiritual joy."

The Pope has spoken often of the suffering of the elderly, including not only their physical discomforts but also their emotional and psychological pain. The family, John Paul always insists, is the source of relief from this pain.

Finally, the Holy Father reminds those facing death of their participation in the death and resurrection of the Lord, that prayer is the source of hope in times of crisis, and that no pain and suffering is greater than that of the spiritual separation from God.

SUFFERING, DYING, AND DEATH

✠ SACRED SCRIPTURE IS A GREAT BOOK ABOUT
suffering.

Apostolic Letter on the Christian Meaning of Holy Suffering, 1984

✠ ALL CONCERN FOR THE SICK AND SUFFERING IS
part of the Church's life and mission. The Church has always understood itself to be charged by Christ with the
care of the poor, the weak, the defenseless, the suffering and
those who mourn. This means that as you alleviate suffering and
seek to heal, you also bear witness to the Christian view of suffering and to the meaning of life and death as taught by your Christian faith.

Homily at Mass in Los Angeles Coliseum, September 15, 1987

✠ THE LETTER TO THE HEBREWS SPEAKS OF
being made perfect through suffering (see Heb 5:8–10).
This is because the purifying flames of trial and sorrow
have the power to transform us from within by unleashing our
love, teaching us compassion for others, and thus drawing us
closer to Christ. Next to her Son, Mary is the most perfect example of this. It is precisely in being the Mother of Sorrows that she is
a mother to each one of us and to all of us. The spiritual sword that
pierces her heart opens up a river of compassion for all who suffer.

Homily at Mass in Los Angeles Coliseum, September 15, 1987

✠ THE FINAL RIDDLE FOR HUMAN BEINGS IS DEATH.
In looking to Christ, man learns that he himself is destined to live. Christ's Eucharist is the pledge of life. The

one who eats Christ's flesh and drinks His blood already has eternal life (see Jn 6:54). Finally, in conquering death by His Resurrection, Christ reveals the resurrection of all; He proclaims life and reveals man to himself in his final destiny, which is life.

Ad Limina *Address to Bishops from*
Los Angeles and San Francisco,
July 8, 1988

✠ CHRIST TOOK UPON HIMSELF THE WHOLE OF human suffering and radically transformed it through the Paschal Mystery of His Passion, Death and Resurrection. The triumph of the Cross gives human suffering a new dimension, a redemptive value.

Homily at Mass in Los Angeles Coliseum,
September 15, 1987

✠ [THE ELDERLY] ARE SOMETIMES FORSAKEN. They suffer because of their old age. They also suffer because of the various troubles that advanced age brings with it. But their greatest suffering is when they do not find the due understanding and gratitude on the part of those from whom they are entitled to expect it.

The Family: Center of Love and Life
General Audience, December 31, 1978

✠ WE LIVE IN THIS WORLD, *WITH THE INEVITABLE prospect of death,* right from the moment of conception and of birth. And yet we must look beyond the material aspect of our earthly existence. Certainly, bodily death is a necessary passage for us all; but it is also true that what from its very beginning has borne in itself the very image and likeness of God cannot be completely given back to the corruptible matter of the universe. This is a fundamental truth and attitude of our Christian faith.

Homily at San Antonio, Texas, September 13, 1987

✠ SUFFERING, IN FACT, IS ALWAYS A TRIAL — AT times a very hard one — to which humanity is subjected.

Apostolic Letter on the Christian Meaning of
Holy Suffering, 1984

✠ THE SO-CALLED QUALITY OF LIFE IS INTERPRETED primarily or exclusively as economic efficiency, inordinate consumerism, physical beauty and pleasure, to the neglect of the more profound dimensions — interpersonal, spiritual and religious — of existence. In such a context suffering, an inescapable burden of human existence but also a factor of possible personal growth, is "censored," rejected as useless, indeed opposed as an evil always and in every way to be avoided. When it cannot be avoided and the prospect of even some future well-being vanishes, then life appears to have lost all meaning and the temptation grows in man to claim the right to suppress it.

*Encyclical: The Gospel of Life (*Evangelium Vitae), 1995*

✠ IT CAN BE SAID THAT MAN SUFFERS WHENEVER he experiences any kind of evil. In the Old Testament, suffering and evil are identified with each other.

Apostolic Letter on the Christian Meaning of
Holy Suffering, 1984

✠ IN OLD AGE, HOW SHOULD ONE FACE THE INEVITABLE decline of life? How should one act in the face of death? The believer knows that his life is in the hands of

God: "You, O Lord, hold my lot" (cf. Ps 16:5), and he accepts from God the need to die: "This is the decree from the Lord for all flesh, and how can you reject the good pleasure of the Most High?" (cf. Sir 41:3–4). Man is not the master of life, nor is he the master of death. In life and in death, he has to entrust himself completely to the "good pleasure of the Most High," to His loving plan.

*Encyclical: The Gospel of Life (*Evangelium Vitae*), 1995*

✠ GOD IS ON THE SIDE OF THE OPPRESSED. HE is beside the parents who cry for their murdered children; He hears the impotent cry of the defenseless and down-trodden; He is in solidarity with women humiliatingly violated; He is near to refugees forced to leave their land and their homes. Do not forget the sufferings of families, of the elderly, widows, the young and children. It is His people who are dying.

Homily at the Mass for Sarajevo at Castel Gandolfo,
September 8, 1994

✠ DEAR FRIENDS! IN WHAT HAPPENED TO THE child of Bethlehem you can recognize what happens to children throughout the world. It is true that a child represents not only the joy of its parents but also the joy of the Church and the whole of society. But it is also true that in our days, unfortunately, many children in different parts of the world are suffering and being threatened: they are hungry and poor, they are dying from diseases and malnutrition, they are the victims of war, they are abandoned by their parents and condemned to remain without a home, without the warmth of a family of their own, they suffer many forms of violence and arrogance from grown-ups. How can we not care, when we see the suffering of so many children, especially when this suffering is in some way caused by grown-ups.

Christmas Letter to the World's Children, December 15, 1994

✠ WHEN WE HAVE STRIVEN TO ALLEVIATE OR overcome suffering, when like Christ we have prayed that "the cup pass us by" (cf. Mt 26:39), and yet suffering remains, then we must walk "the royal road" of the Cross. As I mentioned before, Christ's answer to our question "why?" is above all a call, a vocation. Christ does not give us an abstract answer, but rather He says, "Follow me!" He offers us the opportunity through suffering to take part in His own work of saving the world. And when we do take up our cross, then gradually the salvific meaning of suffering is revealed to us. It is then that in our sufferings we find inner peace and even spiritual joy.

Homily at Mass in Los Angeles Coliseum, September 15, 1987

✠ THE CHURCH PRAYS FOR THE HEALTH OF ALL THE sick, of all the suffering, of all the incurables humanly condemned to irreversible infirmity. She prays *for* the sick, and she prays *with* the sick. She is extremely grateful for every cure, even if it is partial and gradual. And at the same time, with her whole attitude she makes it understood—like Christ— that cure is something exceptional, that from the point of view of the divine "economy" of salvation it is an extraordinary and almost "supplementary" fact.

Homily at St. Peters, February 11, 1979

✠ DEATH IS NOT ONLY A "NATURAL" NECESSITY. Death is a mystery. Here we enter the particular time in which the whole Church, more than ever, wishes to meditate on death as the mystery of man in Christ. Christ the son of God accepted death as a natural necessity, as an inevitable part of man's fate on earth. Jesus Christ accepted death as the consequence of sin. Right from the beginning death was united with sin: the death of the body ("to dust you shall return") and the death of the human spirit owing to disobedience to God, to the

Holy Spirit. Jesus Christ accepted death as a sign of obedience to God, in order to restore to the human spirit the full gift of the Holy Spirit. Jesus Christ accepted death to overcome sin. Jesus Christ accepted death to overcome death in the very essence of its perennial mystery.

Ash Wednesday Address, March 1979

✠ PAIN AND SORROW ARE NOT ENDURED ALONE or in vain. Although it remains difficult to understand suffering, Jesus has made it clear that its value is linked to His own suffering and death, to His own sacrifice. In other words, by your suffering you help Jesus in His work of salvation. Your call to suffering requires strong faith and patience. Yes, it means that you are called to love with a special intensity. But remember that our Blessed Mother Mary is close to you, just as she was close to Jesus at the foot of the Cross. And she will never leave you all alone.

Address at Dublin, September 29, 1979

✠ EARTHLY SUFFERING, WHEN ACCEPTED IN LOVE, is like a bitter kernel containing the seed of new life, the treasure of divine glory to be given man in eternity.

Vatican Address, April 27, 1994

✠ ESPECIALLY THOSE WHO ARE OPPRESSED BY apparently senseless moral suffering find in Jesus' moral suffering the meaning of their own trials, and they go with Him into Gethsemani. In Him they find the strength to accept pain with holy abandon and trusting obedience to the Father's will. And they feel rising from within their hearts the prayer of Gethsemani: "But let it be as you would have it, Father, not as I" (Mk 14:36). They mystically identify with Jesus' resolve when He was arrested: "Am I not to drink the cup the Father has given me?" (Jn 18:11). In Christ they also find the courage to offer their pain for the salvation of all, having learned the mysterious fruit-fulness of every sacrifice from the offering on Calvary, according to the principle set forth by Jesus: "I solemnly assure you, unless the grain of wheat falls to the earth and dies, it remains just a grain of wheat. But if it dies, it produces much fruit" (Jn 12:24).

Vatican Address, April 27, 1994

MAN WHO, ACCORDING TO THE LAWS OF NATURE, is "condemned to death," man who lives in the perspective of the annihilation of his body, exists at the same time in the perspective of future life, and is called to joy.

The solemnity of All Saints puts before the eyes of our faith all those who have already reached the fullness of their call to union with God. The day that commemorates the dead directs our thoughts toward those who, having left this world, are waiting in expiation to reach that fullness of love which union with God requires.

Vatican Address, November 1, 1978

THE POPE WISHES TO GIVE SPECIAL ATTENTION to the sick, to bring them an affectionate greeting and a word of comfort and encouragement. You, dear sick people, have an important place in the Church, if you can interpret your difficult situation in the light of faith and if, in this light, you are able to live your illness with a generous and strong heart. Each of you can then affirm with St. Paul: "In my flesh I complete what is lacking in Christ's afflictions for the sake of his body, that is, the church" (Col 1:24).

Vatican Address, November 19, 1978

✠ WE DIE IN THE PHYSICAL BODY WHEN ALL THE energies of life are extinguished. We die through sin when love dies in us. Outside of love there is no life. If man opposes love and lives without love, death takes root in his soul and grows. For this reason Christ cries out: "I give you a new commandment: Love one another. Such as my love has been for you, so must your love be for each other" (Jn 13:34). The cry for love is the cry for life, for the victory of the soul over sin and death. The source of this victory is the Cross of Jesus Christ: His Death and His Resurrection.

Homily at San Antonio, Texas, September 13, 1987

✠ BROTHERS IN CHRIST, WHO KNOW THE BITTER harshness of the way of the Cross, do not feel that you are alone. The Church is with you as a sacrament of salvation to sustain you in your difficult path. She receives much when you live your suffering with faith; she is beside you with the comfort of active solidarity in her members so that you never lose hope. Remember how Jesus invites you: "Come to me all of you who are weary and tired, and I will give you complete rest" (Mt 11:28).

Address at the Vatican AIDS Conference, November 30, 1989

THE UNIVERSAL
CHURCH

THE CHURCH IS UNIVERSAL BECAUSE IT HAS SOME-
thing to offer all peoples, and welcomes all countries and cultures into its institutions. The revelation of God in Jesus Christ is
subject to no boundaries. Christ is salvation for all humanity.

In another sense, the Catholic Church is universal for what
it embodies. Its highest governing body includes representatives
from nearly all nations and races. Its churches span the world,
from small villages in the remotest parts of Africa to the largest
cities in the Western world. Because its truths are universal, its
mission is universal as well. The Church's history has touched
and will continue to touch the histories of countries and cultures
throughout the world.

These are some of the reasons why churches can never be
considered individually—they each form a part of a universal

physical and spiritual entity. For Pope John Paul II, any church severed from its roots in the universal Church is incomplete. As members of one body, individual churches contribute to the growth of the universal Church by developing its particular gifts. In return, the universal Church enriches individual churches through its collective experience.

THE UNIVERSAL CHURCH

✠ THE SPECIFIC CONTRIBUTION OF THE CHURCH—
of her members and of her individual communities—to
the cause of a new humanism, of true human culture, is
the full truth of Christ about humanity: the meaning of humanity, its origin, its destiny and, therefore, its incomparable dignity.

Easter Message from the Vatican to
the Bishops of the United States, April 3, 1983

✠ JESUS CHRIST TAUGHT THAT MAN NOT ONLY
receives and experiences the mercy of God, but that he is
also called "to practice mercy" toward others: "Blessed are
the merciful, for they shall obtain mercy." The Church sees in
these words a call to action, and she tries to practice mercy. All
the beatitudes of the Sermon on the Mount indicate the way of
conversion and of reform of life, but the one referring to those
who are merciful is particularly eloquent in this regard. Man attains to the merciful love of God, His mercy, to the extent that he
himself is interiorly transformed in the spirit of that love toward
his neighbor.

Encyclical: Mercy of God
(Dives in Misericordia), 1980

✠ FOLLOWING CHRIST, THE CHURCH SEEKS THE
truth, which is not always the same as the majority opinion. She listens to conscience and not to power, and in
this way she defends the poor and the downtrodden.

Apostolic Exhortation Familiaris Consortio, 1981

✠ WHILE REMAINING FAITHFUL TO HER DOCTRINE and discipline, the Church esteems and honors all cultures; she respects them in all her evangelizing efforts among the various peoples. At the first Pentecost, those present heard the Apostles speaking in their own languages (see Acts 2:4ff.). With the guidance of the Holy Spirit, we try in every age to bring the Gospel convincingly and understandably to people of all races, languages and cultures. It is important to realize that there is no black Church, no white Church, no American Church; but there is and must be, in the one Church of Jesus Christ, a home for blacks, whites, Americans, every culture and race.

Address at Meeting with Black Catholic Leadership, New Orleans, September 12, 1987

✠ THE CHURCH LIVES AN AUTHENTIC LIFE WHEN she professes and proclaims mercy—the most stupendous attribute of the Creator and of the Redeemer—and when she brings people close to the sources of the Savior's mercy, of which she is the trustee and dispenser.

Encyclical: Mercy of God (Dives in Misericordia), 1980

✠ THE CATHOLIC CHURCH IS NOT CONFINED TO a particular territory and she has no geographical borders; her members are men and women of all regions of the world. She knows, from many centuries of experience, that suppression, violation or restriction of religious freedom has caused suffering, bitterness, moral and material hardship, and that even today there are millions of people enduring these evils. By contrast, the recognition, guarantee and respect of religious freedom bring serenity to individuals and peace to the social community; they also represent an important factor in strengthening a nation's moral cohesion, in improving people's common welfare and in enriching the cooperation among nations in an atmosphere of mutual trust.

The Freedom of Conscience and Religions, September 1, 1980

✠ RESIST THE TEMPTATION OF WHATEVER CAN weaken communion in the Church as a sacrament of unity and salvation—whether it be from those who make an ideology of the faith or claim to build a "popular Church" which is not that of Christ, or whether it be from those who promote the spread of religious sects which have little to do with the true contents of the faith.

Message Delivered at Santo Domingo, Dominican Republic, October 12, 1984

✠ NOW THIS IS THE ONLY MOTIVE THAT THE Church—and with her the Pope at this moment—has before her eyes and in her heart: that every man may meet Christ in order that Christ may walk with every man along the ways of life.

Address at Rio de Janeiro, July 10, 1980

✠ THE PRESENT TIME IS AN IMPORTANT MOMENT in the history of the universal Church and, in particular, of the Church in Ireland. So many things have changed. So many valuable new insights have been gained in what it means to be Christian. So many new problems have to be faced by the faithful, either because of the increased pace of change in society or because of the new demands that are made on the people of God—demands to live to the fullest the mission of evangelization.

Homily at the Shrine of Our Lady of Knock, Ireland, January 1, 1979

✠ Universal by nature, [the Catholic Church] is conscious of being at the service of all and never identifies with any one national community. She welcomes to her bosom all nations, races and cultures. She is mindful of—indeed she knows that she is the depository of—God's design for humanity: to gather all people into one family. And this because God is the Creator and Father of all. That is the reason why every time that Christianity—whether according to its Western or Eastern tradition—becomes the instrument of a form of nationalism, it is, as it were, wounded in its very heart and made sterile.

The Risks Attached to Nationalism
Address to Diplomats, January 15, 1994

✠ The Church sheds light upon temporal realities; she purifies, uplifts and reconciles them to God. This she does, on the one hand, through the presence and action of her members in the world of human affairs and human endeavors. Countless works and institutions, large and small, in every corner of the world testify to the ecclesial community's unfailing commitment and generosity in serving the good of the human family and in meeting the needs of millions of our brothers and sisters. This boundless witness of faith and love on the part of single members of the Church as well as of groups and communities reveals the true face of the Church to the world. It is the fulfillment of Jesus' pressing invitation: "Let your light so shine before men, that they may see your good works and give glory to your Father who is in heaven" (Mt 5:16).

Reflections on the New Encyclical
Ad Limina *Address, October 15, 1993*

✠ The approaching end of the second millennium demands of everyone an examination of conscience and the promotion of fitting ecumenical initiatives so that we can celebrate the Great Jubilee, if not completely united, at least much closer to overcoming the divisions of the second millennium.

Tertio Millennio Adveniente: Apostolic Letter for the Jubilee 2000

✠ HOW MANY TESTIMONIES OF FAITH, HOW MANY messages of fidelity I have received from communities throughout China! Bishops, priests, religious and lay people have wished to reaffirm their unshakable and full communion with Peter and the rest of the Church. As pastor of the universal Church, my heart greatly rejoices at this. I earnestly invite you all to seek paths to communion and reconciliation, paths which draw their light and inspiration from the truth Himself: Jesus Christ.

Message Broadcast to Catholics in China, January 14, 1995

✠ THE SECOND VATICAN COUNCIL REFERS TO THE Church as a mystery—a mystery of communion. This means that the Church is more than just a community or tradition with shared beliefs and practices, more than an organization with moral influence. Using the imagery of Scripture, the Council also speaks of the Church as a sheepfold, a cultivated field and a building. The Church is Christ's Body, His Bride, and our Mother. We believe that our communion with Christ and with one another comes into being through the outpouring of the Holy Spirit. We believe too that the Holy Spirit makes it fruitful.

Address at Detroit, September 18, 1987

✠ THE UNIVERSAL DIMENSION AND THE PARTICULAR dimension constitute two essential sources in the life of the Church: communion and diversity, tradition and new times, the ancient Christian lands and new people coming to the faith. The Church has succeeded in being one, and at the same time differentiated. Accepting unity as the first principle, she has taken on different forms in the individual parts of the world. This is true in a particular way for the Western Church and for the Eastern Church before their progressive estrangement from each other.

Apostolic Letter Euntes in Mundum (*Go into All The World*), 1988

✠ THE "NEW EVANGELIZATION," WHICH THE modern world urgently needs and which I have emphasized many times, must include among its essential elements a proclamation of the Church's social doctrine. As in the days of Pope Leo XIII, this doctrine is still suitable for indicating the right way to respond to the great challenges of today, when ideologies are being increasingly discredited. Now, as then, we need to repeat that there can be no genuine solution of the "social question" apart from the Gospel, and that the "new things" can find in the Gospel the context for their correct understanding and the proper moral perspective for judgment on them.

Encyclical: The One Hundredth Year (Centesimus Annus), 1991

✠ THE MOST VALUABLE GIFT THAT THE CHURCH can offer to the bewildered and restless world of our time is to form within it Christians who are confirmed in what is essential and who are humbly joyful in their faith. Catechesis will teach this to them, and it will itself be the first to benefit from it: "The man who wishes to understand himself thoroughly—and not just in accordance with immediate, partial, often superficial, and even illusory standards and measures of his being—must come to Christ with his unrest and uncertainty, and even his weakness and sinfulness, his life and death. He must, so to speak, enter into Christ with all his own self; he must 'appropriate' Christ and assimilate the whole of the reality of the Incarnation and redemption in order to find himself."

Catechism in Our Time, October 1979

✠ FINALLY, DEAR FRIENDS, I THINK OF YOUR insertion into the universal Church. It is a beautiful and great mystery. The tree of the Church, planted by Jesus in the Holy Land, has not stopped developing. All the countries of the old Roman Empire were grafted onto it. My own Polish homeland experienced its hour of evangelization and the Church of Poland has been grafted onto the tree of the Church in order to make it produce new fruits. And now your community of Congolese believers has in its turn been grafted onto the tree of the Church.

Homily in the Congo, May 5, 1980

✠ WHEN THE CHURCH PROCLAIMS GOD'S salvation to man, when she offers and communicates the life of God through the sacraments, when she gives direction to human life through the commandments of love of God and neighbor, she contributes to the enrichment of human dignity. But just as the Church can never abandon her religious and transcendent mission on behalf of man, so too she is aware that today her activity meets with particular difficulties and obstacles. That is why she devotes herself with ever new energies and methods to an evangelization which promotes the whole human being. Even on the eve of the third millennium, she continues to be "a sign and safeguard of the transcendence of the human person" as indeed she always sought to be.

Encyclical: The One Hundredth Year (Centesimus Annus), 1991

WOMEN

JOHN PAUL BELIEVES THAT WOMEN HAVE A DIGNITY AND responsibility that is in every way equal to that of men and that closing any public role to them is contrary to the proper position of women in the world. At the same time, he insists that clear recognition be given to the value of the role of women as wives and mothers. This belief in no way contradicts his conviction that women and men are equal in the workplace. Neither men nor women can ignore the family in favor of work. John Paul also believes that society must be restructured so that women do not have to choose between work and family—that is, he feels that women's rightful place in the world of work should not have to be purchased at the cost of family.

The differences that the Holy Father acknowledges between men and women do not imply the acceptance of male domination. In fact, any domination of one person by another is not a natural state at all, but a product of original sin. Discrimination against women, like other types of discrimination, has its roots in the inability to understand and acknowledge that every human being is a child of God.

However firm his belief in the equality of the sexes, the Pope remains a traditionalist. He believes that the choice to remain a virgin or to become a mother is equally worthy, that women cannot be ordained in the priesthood, and that Mary is the model mother and the model woman.

WOMEN

✝ IT MUST BE CLEAR THAT THE CHURCH STANDS
firmly against every form of discrimination which in any
way compromises the equal dignity of women and men.
The complete equality of persons is, however, accompanied by
a marvelous complementarity. This complementarity concerns
not only the roles of men and women but also, and more deeply,
their makeup and meaning as persons.

Women's Roles Discussed with Members of Mother Mary
MacKillop's Order in Australia, January 19, 1995

✝ IN DEALING WITH THE SPECIFIC RIGHTS OF
women as women, it is necessary to return again and again
to the immutable basis of Christian anthropology as it is
foreshadowed in the Scriptural account of the creation of man—
as male and female—in the image and likeness of God. Both man
and woman are created in the image of the personhood of God,
with inalienable personal dignity, and in complementarity one
with the other. Whatever violates the complementarity of women
and men, whatever impedes the true communion of persons according to the complementarity of the sexes offends the dignity of
both women and men.

Speech to the Bishops of the United States,
September 2, 1988

✝ TOIL IS SOMETHING THAT IS UNIVERSALLY
known, for it is universally experienced. It is familiar to
women who, sometimes without proper recognition on
the part of society, and even of their own families, bear the daily

burden and responsibility for their homes and the upbringing of their children.

Encyclical: On Human Work (Laborem Exercens), 1981

✠ As I have stated, and as Archbishop Weakland has pointed out, women are not called to the priesthood. Although the teaching of the Church on this point is quite clear, it in no way alters the fact that women are indeed an essential part of the Gospel plan to spread the Good News of the Kingdom. And the Church is irrevocably committed to this truth.

Speech to Bishops at Los Angeles, September 1987

✠ I am convinced that a mistaken anthropology is at the root of the failure of society to understand the Church teaching on the true role of women. That role is in no way diminished but is in fact enhanced by being related in a special way to motherhood—the source of new life—both physical and spiritual.

Women's Roles Discussed with Members of Mother Mary
MacKillop's Order in Australia, January 19, 1995

✠ It is a sad reflection on the human condition that still today, at the end of the twentieth century, it is necessary to affirm that every woman is equal in dignity to man and a full member of the human family within which she has a distinctive place and vocation that is complementary to but in no way less valuable than man's. In much of the world much still has to be done to meet the educational and health needs of girls and young women so that they may achieve their full potential in society.

Cairo Population Conference Draft Document Criticized,
March 3, 1994

✠ JESUS ALWAYS SHOWED THE GREATEST ESTEEM
and the greatest respect for woman, for every woman, and
in particular He was sensitive to female suffering. Going
beyond the religious and social barriers of the time, Jesus reestablished woman in her full dignity as a human person before God
and before men.

Thoughts on Women
Address to Italian Maids, April 29, 1979

✠ WHEN WOMEN ARE ABLE FULLY TO SHARE THEIR
gifts with the whole community, the very way in which society understands and organizes itself is improved and
comes to reflect in a better way the substantial unity of the
human family. Here we see the most important condition for the
consolidation of authentic peace. The growing presence of
women in social, economic and political life at the local, national
and international levels is thus a very positive development.

Women: Teachers of Peace, January 1, 1995

✠ IN ORDER TO BE A TEACHER OF PEACE, A WOMAN
must first of all nurture peace within herself. Inner peace
comes from knowing that one is loved by God and from
the desire to respond to His love. History is filled with marvelous
examples of women who, sustained by this knowledge, have been
able successfully to deal with difficult situations of exploitation,
discrimination, violence and war.

Women: Teachers of Peace, January 1, 1995

✠ MANY WOMEN, ESPECIALLY AS A RESULT OF
social and cultural conditioning, do not become fully
aware of their dignity. Others are victims of a materialistic
and hedonistic outlook which views them as mere objects of pleasure and does not hesitate to organize the exploitation of women,

even of young girls, into a despicable trade. Special concern needs to be shown for these women, particularly by other women who, thanks to their own upbringing and sensitivity, are able to help them discover their own inner worth and resources. Women need to help women and to find support in the valuable and effective contributions which associations, movements and groups, many of them of a religious character, have proved capable of making in this regard.

Women: Teachers of Peace, January 1, 1995

✠ SOCIETY SHOULD NOT ALLOW WOMAN'S MATERnal role to be demeaned or count as of little value in comparison with other possibilities. Greater consideration should be given to the social role of mothers, and support should be given to programs which aim at decreasing maternal mortality, providing prenatal and perinatal care, meeting the nutritional needs of pregnant women and nursing mothers, and helping mothers themselves to provide preventive health care for their infants. In this regard, attention should be given to the positive benefits of breast-feeding for nourishment and disease prevention in infants as well as for maternal bonding and birth spacing.

Cairo Population Conference Draft Document Criticized,
March 3, 1994

✠ THE LEGITIMATE DESIRE TO CONTRIBUTE WITH her own abilities to the common good and the social and economic context itself often brings woman to undertake a professional activity. However, it is necessary to avoid the risk that the family and humanity suffer a loss which impoverishes them, since woman can never be replaced in begetting and rearing children. The authorities should therefore provide for the professional promotion of woman and at the same time safeguard her vocation as a mother and educator with appropriate legislation.

Vatican Address, April 24, 1994

✠ MOTHERHOOD IS WOMAN'S VOCATION. IT IS AN eternal vocation, and it is also a contemporary vocation. "The Mother who understands everything and embraces each of us with her heart": these are the words of a song, sung by young people in Poland, which come into my mind at this moment. The song goes on to announce that today the world is particularly "hungry and thirsty" for that motherhood, which is woman's vocation "physically" and "spiritually," as it is Mary's.

Everything must be done in order that the dignity of this splendid vocation may not be broken in the inner life of the new generations; in order that the authority of the woman-mother may not be diminished in the family, social and public life, and in the whole of our civilization; in all our contemporary legislations, in the organization of work, in publications, in the culture of everyday life, in education and in study: in every field of life.

Vatican Address, January 10, 1979

✠ FOR WOMAN THIS TASK OF HANDING ON THE faith is not meant to be carried out only in the family, but—as we read in *Christifideles Laici:* "also in the various educational environments and, in broader terms, in all that concerns embracing the word of God, its understanding and its communication, as well as its study, research and theological teaching." These are all indications of the role women have in the field of catechesis, which today has spread into broad and diverse areas, some of which were unthinkable in times past.

Vatican Address, July 13, 1994

✟ THE PRESENCE AND THE ROLE OF WOMEN IN the life and mission of the Church, although not linked to the ministerial priesthood, remain absolutely necessary and irreplaceable. As the declaration *Inter Insigniores* points out, "the Church desires that Christian women should become fully aware of the greatness of their mission: today their role is of capital importance both for the renewal and humanization of society and for the rediscovery by believers of the true face of the Church."

Apostolic Letter Ordinatio Sacerdotalis, 1994

✟ WHILE IT MUST BE RECOGNIZED THAT WOMEN have the same right as I to perform various public functions, society must be structured in such a way that wives and mothers are not in practice compelled to work outside the home, and that their families can live and prosper in a dignified way even when they themselves devote their full time to their own family.

Furthermore, the mentality which honors women more for their work outside the home than for their work within the family must be overcome. This requires that men should truly esteem and love women with total respect for their personal dignity, and that society should create and develop conditions favoring work in the home.

Apostolic Exhortation Familiaris Consortio, 1981

WORK

"WORK IS MADE FOR MAN, NOT MAN FOR WORK." This is the principle that guides Pope John Paul's thinking about the place of labor in human life. Human work is the unique way that men and women collaborate with God and participate in God's transforming work. Human beings alone share this special role as cocreators with God of this redeemed but unfinished world. Yet the development of the world by human activity is less important than the self-realization and sanctification meant to be accomplished through it. We work together in a community guided by God's word and animated by God's love. Work is so much more than a means to an end, for in our work we co-create the world with God. Thus work becomes a divine activity, a unifying, sacred, and transforming force.

There is a danger, however, that work may be perverted. Forced work has no dignity, and imposing work on others against their will is ungodly; useless work can be used as punishment;

people can be made into machines and worked to exhaustion, or otherwise have their human worth denied by the work they do. In order for work to be sacred, it must be undertaken with free will and in full understanding of its meaning. John Paul urges us to make no distinctions that declare one kind of work more dignified and worthy than another. In this the Lord Himself set the example: "The greatest among you shall serve the rest."

That all work is sacred has practical consequences for John Paul. The Holy Father insists that workers be sufficiently recompensed so that they can provide for themselves and their families, and he encourages minimum wages, health care benefits, pensions, and sick pay as essential parts of the remuneration for any proper work honestly undertaken and worthy of human labor.

WORK

✝ FOR MAN AND WOMAN THUS CREATED AND commissioned by God, the ordinary working day has great and wonderful significance. People's ideas, activities and undertakings—however commonplace they may be—are used by the Creator to renew the world, to lead it to salvation, to make it a more perfect instrument of divine glory.

Encyclical: On Human Work (Laborem Exercens), 1981

✝ IN VIEW OF THIS SITUATION, WE MUST FIRST OF all recall a principle that has always been taught by the Church: the principle of the priority of labor over capital.

Encyclical: On Human Work (Laborem Exercens), 1981

✝ BOTH THE ORIGINAL INDUSTRIALIZATION THAT gave rise to what is called the worker question and the subsequent industrial and postindustrial changes show in an eloquent manner that, even in the age of ever more mechanized "work," the proper subject of work continues to be man.

Encyclical: On Human Work (Laborem Exercens), 1981

✝ THE DANGER OF TREATING WORK AS A SPECIAL kind of merchandise, or as an impersonal "force" needed for production (the expression "workforce" is, in fact, in common use), always exists, especially when the whole way of looking at the question of economics is marked by the premises of materialistic economism.

Encyclical: On Human Work (Laborem Exercens), 1981

✝ WORK CONSTITUTES A FOUNDATION FOR THE formation of family life, which is a natural right and something that man is called to. These two spheres of values must be properly united and must properly permeate each other.

Encyclical: On Human Work (Laborem Exercens), 1981

✝ THE CHURCH CONSIDERS IT HER DUTY TO speak out on work from the viewpoint of its human value and of the moral order to which it belongs, and she sees this as one of her important tasks within the service that she renders to the evangelical message as a whole.

At the same time she sees it as her particular duty to form a spirituality of work which will help all people to come closer, through work, to God, the creator and redeemer, to participate in His salvific plan for man and the world and to deepen their friendship with Christ in their lives by accepting, through faith, a living participation in His threefold mission as priest, prophet and king, as the Second Vatican Council so eloquently teaches.

Encyclical: On Human Work (Laborem Exercens), 1981

✝ GOD'S REVELATION IS PROFOUNDLY MARKED BY the fundamental truth that man, created in the image of God, shares by his work in the activity of the Creator and that, within the limits of his own human capabilities, man in a sense continues to develop that activity, and perfects it as he advances further and further in the discovery of the resources and values contained in the whole of creation. We find this truth at the very beginning of Sacred Scripture, in the Book of Genesis, where the creation activity itself is presented in the form of "work" done by God during "six days," "resting" on the seventh day.

Encyclical: On Human Work (Laborem Exercens), 1981

✠ THE KNOWLEDGE THAT BY MEANS OF WORK man shares in the work of creation constitutes the most profound motive for undertaking it in various sectors. "The faithful, therefore," we read in the constitution *Lumen Gentium*, "must learn the deepest meaning and the value of all creation, and its orientation to the praise of God. Even by their secular activity they must assist one another to live holier lives."

Encyclical: On Human Work (Laborem Exercens), *1981*

✠ THE VALUE OF WORK DOES NOT END WITH THE individual. The full meaning of work can only be understood in relation to the family and society as well. Work supports and gives stability to the family. Within the family, moreover, children first learn the human and positive meaning of work and responsibility. In each community and in the nation as a whole, work has a fundamental social meaning. It can, moreover, either join people in the solidarity of a shared commitment or set them at odds through exaggerated competition, exploitation and social conflict. Work is a key to the whole social question, when that "question" is understood to be concerned with making work more human.

Homily, Mass at Los Angeles, September 17, 1987

✠ [WORK] IS NOT ONLY GOOD IN THE SENSE THAT it is useful or something to enjoy; it is also good as being something worthy, that is to say, something that corresponds to man's dignity, that expresses this dignity and increases it. If one wishes to define more clearly the ethical meaning of work, that is the truth that one must particularly keep in mind. Work is a good thing for man—a good thing for his humanity—because through work man not only transforms nature, adapting it to his own needs, but he also achieves fulfillment as a human being and indeed, in a sense, becomes "more a human being."

Encyclical: On Human Work (Laborem Exercens), *1981*

✠ WORK IS AN OBLIGATION, THAT IS TO SAY, A DUTY, on the part of man. This is true in all the many meanings of the word. Man must work, both because the Creator has commanded it and because of his own humanity, which requires work in order to be maintained and developed. Man must work out of regard for others, especially his own family, but also for the society he belongs to, the country of which he is a child, and the whole human family of which he is a member, since he is the heir to the work of generations and at the same time a sharer in building the future of those who will come after him in the succession of history. All this constitutes the moral obligation of work, understood in its wide sense.

Encyclical: On Human Work (Laborem Exercens), *1981*

✠ AS WE VIEW THE WHOLE HUMAN FAMILY throughout the world, we cannot fail to be struck by a disconcerting fact of immense proportions: the fact that, while conspicuous natural resources remain unused, there are huge numbers of people who are unemployed or underemployed and countless multitudes of people suffering from hunger. This is a fact that without any doubt demonstrates that both within the individual political communities and in their relationships on the continental and world level there is something wrong with the organization of work and employment, precisely at the most critical and socially most important points.

Encyclical: On Human Work (Laborem Exercens), *1981*

✠ EMIGRATION IN SEARCH OF WORK MUST IN NO way become an opportunity for financial or social exploitation. As regards the work relationship, the same criteria should be applied to immigrant workers as to all other workers in the society concerned. The value of work should be measured by the same standard and not according to the difference in nationality, religion or race. For even greater reason the situation of constraint in which the emigrant may find himself should not be exploited.

Encyclical: On Human Work (Laborem Exercens), 1981

✝ THE TRUE ADVANCEMENT OF WOMEN REQUIRES that labor should be structured in such a way that women do not have to pay for their advancement by abandoning what is specific to them and at the expense of the family, in which women as mothers have an irreplaceable role.

Encyclical: On Human Work (Laborem Exercens), 1981

✝ THE CHURCH IS CONVINCED THAT WORK IS A fundamental dimension of man's existence on earth.

Encyclical: On Human Work (Laborem Exercens), 1981

dispute that seems without a solution, tomorrow—if people only
want it!—tomorrow a crossroads of reconciliation and peace.

Homily at Otranto, Italy, October 5, 1980

✠ CONSIDERING HISTORY IN THE LIGHT OF THE
principles of faith in God, we must also reflect on the
catastrophic event of the Shoah, that ruthless and inhu-
man attempt to exterminate the Jewish people in Europe, an
attempt that resulted in millions of victims—including women
and children, the elderly and the sick—exterminated only because they were Jews. Considering the mystery of the suffering
of Israel's children, their witness of hope, of faith and of humanity under dehumanizing outrages, the Church experiences
ever more deeply her common bond with the Jewish people
and with their treasure of spiritual riches in the past and in the
present.

Address at Miami, September 10, 1987

✠ YOUR NATIVE CULTURES ARE THE WEALTH OF
the peoples, effective ways for transmitting the faith, representations of your relation with God, with men and
with the world. They therefore deserve the greatest respect, esteem, sympathy and support on the part of all mankind. These
cultures, in fact, have left remarkable monuments—such as those
of the Maya, Aztecs, Incas and many others—which we still con-
template today with wonder.

Message to Peasants, Quezaltenango, Guatemala,
March 7, 1983

✠ THE POWER OF TRUTH LEADS US TO RECOGNIZE
with Mahatma Gandhi the dignity, equality and fraternal
solidarity of all human beings, and it prompts us to reject

every form of discrimination. It shows us once again the need for mutual understanding, acceptance and collaboration between religious groups in the pluralist society of modern India and throughout the world.

Address at Rag Ghat, India, January 10, 1986

✠ THE VICTORY OF LIFE OVER DEATH IS WHAT every human being desires. All religions, especially the great religious traditions followed by most of the peoples of Asia, bear witness to how deeply the truth regarding our immortality is inscribed in man's religious consciousness. Man's search for life after death finds definitive fulfillment in the resurrection of Christ. Because the risen Christ is the demonstration of God's response to this deeply felt longing of the human spirit, the Church professes: "I believe in the resurrection of the body and in life everlasting" (Apostles' Creed). The risen Christ assures the men and women of every age that they are called to a life beyond the frontier of death.

Address to Manila World Youth Day, January 14, 1995

✠ SHINTOISM, THE TRADITIONAL RELIGION OF Japan, affirms that all men are equally sons of God and that, because of this, all men are brothers. Moreover, in your religious tradition, you show a special sensitivity and appreciation for the harmony and beauty of nature, and you show a readiness to recognize there a revelation of God the Most High. I am also aware that in your noble teaching on personal asceticism you seek to make the heart of man ever more pure.

The many things that we hold in common impel us to unite ever more closely in friendship and brotherhood in the service of all humanity.

Vatican Address, February 21, 1979

✠ JERUSALEM CONTAINS COMMUNITIES OF believers full of life, whose presence the peoples of the whole world regard as a sign and source of hope—especially those who consider the Holy City to be in a certain way their spiritual heritage and a symbol of peace and harmony. Indeed insofar as she is the homeland of the hearts of all the spiritual descendants of Abraham who hold her very dear, and the place where, according to faith, the created things of earth encounter the infinite transcendence of God, Jerusalem stands out as a symbol of the coming together, or union, and of universal peace for the human family.

Apostolic Letter Redemptionis Anno, 1984

✠ [THE DIALOGUE WITH PEOPLE OF OTHER religions] is a complex of human activities, all founded upon respect and esteem for people of different religions. It includes the daily living together in peace and mutual help, with each bearing witness to the values learned through the experience of faith. It means a readiness to cooperate with others for the betterment of humanity, and a commitment to search together for true peace. It means the encounter of theologians and other religions, areas of convergence and divergence. Where circumstances permit, it means a sharing of spiritual experiences and insights. This sharing can take the form of coming together as brothers and sisters to pray to God in ways which safeguard the uniqueness of each religious tradition.

Address to the Members and Staff of the Secretariat for Non-Christians, April 28, 1987

✠ JUST AS WE CATHOLICS INVITE OUR CHRISTIAN brethren to share in our initiatives, so too we declare that we are ready to collaborate in theirs, and we welcome the invitations presented to us. In this pursuit of integral human development we can also do much with the members of other religions, as in fact is being done in various places.

Encyclical: On Social Concerns (Sollicitudo Rei Socialis), 1987

ALL CHRISTIANS MUST BE COMMITTED TO dialogue with the believers of all religions, so that mutual understanding and collaboration may grow; so that moral values may be strengthened; so that God may be praised in all creation. Ways must be developed to make this dialogue become a reality everywhere, but especially in Asia, the continent that is the cradle of ancient cultures and religions. Likewise the Catholics and the Christians of other churches must join together in the search for full unity, in order that Christ may become ever more manifest in the love of His followers.

Radio Broadcast to Asia from Japan, February 21, 1981

MANY INNOCENT PEOPLE OF DIFFERENT nationalities [died in Nazi concentration camps], but in particular, the children of the Jewish people, for whom the Nazi regime had planned a systematic extermination, suffered the dramatic experience of the Holocaust. The consideration of mitigating circumstances does not exonerate the Church from the obligation to express profound regret for the weaknesses of so many of her sons and daughters who sullied her face.

Speech Marking the Fiftieth Anniversary of the Liberation of Auschwitz, Rome, January 29, 1995

DEAR BROTHERS AND SISTERS OF THESE RELI- gions and every religion: so many people today experience inner emptiness even amid material prosperity, because they overlook the great questions of life: What is man? What is the meaning and purpose of life? What is goodness and what is sin? What gives rise to suffering and what purpose does it serve? What is the path to true happiness? What is death, judgment and retribution after death? What, finally, is that ultimate, ineffable mystery which embraces our existence, from which we take our origin and toward which we move?

These profoundly spiritual questions, which are shared to some degree by all religions, also draw us together in a common concern for man's earthly welfare, especially world peace.

Speech to Interreligious Leaders at Los Angeles, September 16, 1987

YOUTH

POPE JOHN PAUL IS DEVOTED TO CHILDREN AND YOUNG people and has addressed them often, all over the world. Our fondness and regard for children and the young—as measured by our response to their needs—are a test of our regard for human beings in general. No society that does not highly value the young can long survive, and the Pope himself finds a positive delight in the young: "I wish to express," he said, "the joy that we all find in children, the springtime of life, the anticipation of the future." It must also be said that John Paul finds this joy in all children, including the handicapped and the sick, and he encourages parents and others to lavish attention on children with special needs.

For John Paul, the family is at the center of a child's or a young person's life. The family is the single most important provider of education, and the Christian family is the model for a properly ordered society. Especially in industrialized societies, parents may be tempted to evade the responsibility for education,

✠ UNIVERSITY STUDENTS ARE IN A SPLENDID position to take to heart the Gospel invitation to go out of themselves, to reject introversion and to concentrate on the needs of others. Students with the opportunities of higher education can readily grasp the relevance for today of Christ's parable of the rich man and Lazarus (see Lk 16:19ff.), with all of its consequences for humanity. What is at stake is not only the rectitude of individual human hearts but also the whole social order as it touches the spheres of economy, politics and human rights and relations.

Westover Hills, Texas, September 13, 1987

✠ YOU WILL HEAR PEOPLE TELL YOU THAT YOUR religious practices are hopelessly out of date, that they hamper your style and your future, that with everything that social and scientific progress has to offer, you will be able to organize your own lives, and that God has played out His role. Even many religious persons will adopt such attitudes, breathing them in from the surrounding atmosphere without attending to the practical atheism that is at their origin.

Remarks to Youth in Galway, Ireland,
September 30, 1979

✠ YES, DEAR YOUNG PEOPLE, DO NOT CLOSE your eyes to the moral sickness that stalks your society today, and from which your youth alone will not protect you. How many young people have already warped their consciences and have substituted the true joy of life with drugs, sex, alcohol, vandalism and the empty pursuit of mere material possessions.

Remarks to Youth in Galway, Ireland,
September 30, 1979

✠ EACH SUCCESSIVE WORLD YOUTH DAY HAS been a confirmation of young people's openness to the meaning of life as a gift received, a gift to which they are eager to respond by striving for a better world for themselves and their fellow human beings. I believe that we should correctly interpret their deepest aspirations by saying that what they ask is that society—especially the leaders of nations and all who control the destinies of peoples—accept them as true partners in the construction of a more humane, more just, more compassionate world. They ask to be able to contribute their specific ideas and energies to this task.

Remarks at Welcoming Ceremonies
at Regis College, Denver,
August 12, 1993

✠ IN MY PASTORAL VISITS TO THE CHURCH IN every part of the world, I have been deeply moved by the almost universal conditions of difficulty in which young people grow up and live. Too many sufferings are visited upon them by natural calamities, famines, epidemics, by economic and political crises, by the atrocities of wars. And where material conditions are at least adequate, other obstacles arise, not the least of which is the breakdown of family values and stability. In developed countries, a serious moral crisis is already affecting the lives of many young people, leaving them adrift, often without hope and conditioned to look only for instant gratification. Yet everywhere there are young men and women deeply concerned about the world around them, ready to give the best of themselves in service to others and particularly sensitive to life's transcendent meaning.

Remarks at Welcoming Ceremonies
at Regis College, Denver,
August 12, 1993

✝ WE DO NOT ASK THE YOUNG PEOPLE TO ABANDON their uncertainties, questions or criticisms. Rather we ask all those who call themselves Christians to allow themselves to be guided by grace to encounter Christ in the Church, through the sacraments, prayer and the reception of the Word.

International Youth Forum's Message to the World's Youth,
August 26, 1993

✝ YOUNG PEOPLE OF WORLD YOUTH DAY, THE Church asks you to go, in the power of the Holy Spirit, to those who are near and those who are far away. Share with them the freedom you have found in Christ. People thirst for genuine inner freedom. They yearn for the life which Christ came to give in abundance. The world at the approach of a new millennium, for which the whole Church is preparing, is like a field ready for the harvest. Christ needs laborers ready to work in His vineyard. May you, the Catholic young people of the world, not fail Him. In your hands, carry the cross of Christ. On your lips, the words of life. In your hearts, the saving grace of the Lord.

A Celebration of Life
Homily at Cherry Creek State Park, Aurora, Colorado,
August 15, 1993

✝ PARENTS AND OLDER PEOPLE SOMETIMES feel that they have lost contact with you, and they are upset, just as Mary and Joseph felt anguish when they realized that Jesus had stayed behind in Jerusalem. Sometimes you are very critical of the world of adults, and sometimes they are very critical of you. This is not something new, and it is not always without real basis in life. But always remember that you owe your life and upbringing to your parents, and the Fourth Commandment expresses in a concise way the demands of justice toward them (cf. Catechism of the Catholic Church, 2215).

In most cases, they have provided for your education at the cost of personal sacrifice. Thanks to them you have been introduced to the cultural and social heritage of your community and country. Generally speaking, your parents have been your first teachers in the faith. Parents therefore have a right to expect from their sons and daughters the mature fruits of their efforts, just as children and young people have the right to expect from their parents the love and care which lead to a healthy development. I am asking you to build bridges of dialogue and communication with your parents. Be a healthy influence on society to help break down the barriers which have been raised between generations!

Homily for Closing Mass of Manila World Youth Day,
January 15, 1995

✝ WE CANNOT IGNORE THE DEEP DESIRES THAT ARE stirring in people's hearts today. In spite of negative signs, many hunger for an authentic and challenging spirituality. There is "a fresh discovery of God in His transcendent reality as the infinite Spirit," and young people especially are looking for a solid foundation upon which to build their lives. The youth of America look to you to lead them to Christ, who is the only "existentially adequate response to the desire in every human heart for goodness, truth and life." Allow me to repeat what I said to the bishops last month in Denver: "Are we always ready to help the young people discover the transcendent elements of Christian life? From our words and actions do they conclude that the Church is indeed a mystery of communion with the Blessed Trinity and not just a human institution with temporal aims?"

Accompanying Youth in Their Pilgrimage of Faith
Ad Limina *Address, September 21, 1993*

✠ WHAT DO THE CHURCH AND THE POPE EXPECT of the young people of the Tenth World Youth Day? That you confess Jesus Christ. And that you learn to proclaim all that the message of Christ contains for the true liberation and genuine progress of humanity. This is what Christ expects of you. This is what the Church looks for in the young people of the Philippines, of Asia, of the world.

Address to Manila World Youth Day, January 14, 1995

✠ YOUNG PEOPLE, I SAY TO YOU, CHRIST IS WAITING for you with open arms: Christ is relying on you to build justice and peace, to spread love. As in Turin, I say again today: "You must return to the school of Christ to rediscover the true, full, deep meaning of these words. The necessary support for these values lies only in possession of a sure and sincere faith, a faith that embraces God and man, man in God. There is not a more adequate, a deeper dimension to give to this word 'man,' to this word 'love,' to this word 'freedom,' to this word 'peace' and 'justice': there is nothing else, there is only Christ."

Address to the Sacred College of Cardinals, December 22, 1980

✠ WHERE THERE ARE YOUNG PEOPLE, ADOLESCENTS, children, there is the guarantee of joy, since it is life in its most spontaneous and most exuberant bloom. You possess this *joie de vivre* abundantly and bestow it generously on a world that is sometimes tired, discouraged, disheartened, disappointed. This meeting of ours is also a sign of hope, because adults, not only your parents, but also your teachers, professors and all those who collaborate in your physical and intellectual growth and development, see in you those who will attain what they, perhaps—owing to various circumstances—have not been able to achieve.

Vatican Address, November 22, 1978

✠ THERE IS ALWAYS A SPECIAL ATTRACTION IN YOU
young people, because of that instinctive goodness of
yours not contaminated by evil, and because of your particular readiness to accept truth, and put it into practice. And
since God is truth, you, loving and accepting truth, are nearest to
heaven.

Vatican Address, December 13, 1978

✠ COME PARTICULARLY YOU, YOUNG PEOPLE,
thirsty for innocence, contemplation, interior beauty,
pure joy; you who seek the ultimate and decisive meaning
of existence and history, come, and recognize and enjoy Christian and Benedictine spirituality, before letting yourselves be attracted by other experiences!

Address at Monte Cassino Abbey, May 18, 1979

✠ THE CHURCH NEEDS YOU. THE WORLD NEEDS
you, because it needs Christ, and you belong to Christ.
And so I ask you to accept your responsibility in the
Church, the responsibility of your Catholic education: to help —
by your words and, above all, by the example of your lives — to
spread the Gospel. You do this by praying, and by being just and
truthful and pure. Dear young people: by a real Christian life, by
the practice of your religion you are called to give witness to your
faith. And because actions speak louder than words, you are
called to proclaim by the conduct of your daily lives that you
really do believe that Jesus Christ is Lord!

Address in New York City, October 3, 1979

CHRISTIAN LIFE

THE SELECTIONS IN THIS SECTION OFFER A SAMPLING of the wisdom of the Pope on vital themes and aspects of Christian life. These selections include the Arts, Jesus Christ, Celibacy, the Sacraments, Evil, Women Religious, Catholic Education, Mary, Ecumenism, and Easter.

These final selections, of course, do not encompass the vast scope of the Pope's knowledge and interests, not to mention his words in books, speeches, homilies, letters, and encyclicals on an extraordinarily wide range of matters both religious and secular. In his many years as Pope, he has adhered to a punishing schedule, both at the Vatican and abroad on more than sixty trips, throughout all of which he has delivered as many as three memorable addresses a day, almost every day of the year. His collected speeches and addresses alone add up to some twenty volumes (most of which are available in the journal *The Pope Speaks*).

Moreover, before ascending to the papacy, John Paul had been a poet, a playwright, and a drama critic, as well as a philosopher of distinction, none of which vocations have been represented in this collection because of constraints of space and the focus on popular themes and vital questions. Thus, these selections explore various key elements of Christian living and Catholic faith. But any reader can easily think of many more topics that could have been added.

CHRISTIAN LIFE

JESUS CHRIST

✠ CHRIST IS THE ONE AWAITED BY ALL PEOPLES;
He is God's answer to humanity. After the long period of "evangelical preparations" (Eusebius of Cesarea), here He comes from the Father's bosom. He comes to be a man like us, to offer God the supreme act of worship and love which alone could reconcile Him with man.

The Church in the World of the 1980s
Address to Cardinals, Rome, December 22, 1980

✠ JESUS IS THE SON OF GOD "INCARNATE," COME IN
the flesh, in order to live the concrete realities of our existence as man and as the Son of God at the same time. It is an unprecedented mystery. You have an inkling of the dignity that He conferred on your lives as humble workers, since He lived in Nazareth, in Palestine. He lived it under the gaze of God His Father, intimately linked to Him in the action of grace. He offered to God all its joys and all its difficulties. He lived it with simplicity, purity of heart, with courage, as a servant, as a friend welcoming the sick, the afflicted, the poor of every kind, with a love that no one will surpass and which He made His testament: Love one another, as I have loved you. It is that life which, through the trial of His sacrifice offered to free the world from its sins, is now glorified before God.

Homily at Kinsangani, Zaire,
May 29, 1980

✠ WE CANNOT LEARN CHRISTIANITY AS A LESSON
made up of various chapters, but it is always linked with a
person, a living person, Jesus Christ. Jesus Christ is both
guide and model. It is possible to imitate Him in different ways
and in varying degrees to make Him the "rule" of one's own life.

Address to Youth, Paris, June 1, 1980

✠ THE CHURCH HAS ALWAYS TAUGHT AND CON-
tinues to proclaim that God's revelation was brought to
completion in Jesus Christ, who is the fullness of that revelation, and that "no new public revelation is to be expected before the glorious manifestation of Our Lord" (Constitution on
Divine Revelation, 4). The Church evaluates and judges private
revelations by the criterion of conformity with that single public
revelation.

The Message of Fatima, May 13, 1982

MARY

✠ CONSECRATING THE WORLD TO THE IMMACULATE
heart of Mary means drawing near, through the Mother's
intercession, to the very fountain of life that sprang from
Golgotha. This fountain unceasingly pours forth redemption and
grace. In it reparation is made continually for the sins of the
world. It is a ceaseless source of new life and holiness.

The Message of Fatima, May 13, 1982

✠ MARY LIVED AND EXERCISED HER FREEDOM
precisely by giving herself to God and accepting God's gift
within herself. Until the time of His birth, she sheltered in
her womb the Son of God who became man; she raised Him and
enabled Him to grow, and she accompanied Him in that

supreme act of freedom which is the complete sacrifice of His own life. By the gift of herself, Mary entered fully into the plan of God who gives Himself to the world. By accepting and pondering in her heart events which she did not always understand (cf. Lk 2:19), she became the model of all those who hear the word of God and keep it (cf. Lk 11:28), and merited the title of seat of wisdom. This wisdom is Jesus Christ Himself, the eternal Word of God, who perfectly reveals and accomplishes the will of the Father (cf. Heb 10:5–10). To us too she addresses the command she gave to the servants at Cana in Galilee during the marriage feast: "Do whatever he tells you" (Jn 2:5).

Encyclical: The Splendor of Truth (Veritatis Splendor), 1993

MOTHERHOOD MEANS CARING FOR THE LIFE OF the child. Since Mary is the mother of us all, her care for the life of man is universal. The care of a mother embraces her child totally. Mary's motherhood has its beginning in her motherly care for Christ. In Christ, at the foot of the cross, she accepted John, and in John she accepted all of us totally.

The Message of Fatima, May 13, 1982

THE SACRAMENTS

THE EUCHARIST IS ALSO A GREAT CALL TO CONversion. We know that it is an invitation to the banquet; that, by nourishing ourselves on the eucharist, we receive in it the body and blood of Christ, under the appearances of bread and wine. Precisely because of this invitation, the eucharist is and remains the call to conversion. If we receive it as such a call, such an invitation, it brings forth in us its proper fruits. It transforms our lives. It makes us a "new man," a "new creature" (cf. Gal 6:15; Eph 2:15; 2 Cor 5:17). It helps us not to be "overcome by evil, but to overcome evil by good" (cf. Rom 12:21). The eucharist helps love to triumph in us—love over hatred, zeal over indifference.

Homily in Dublin's Phoenix Park,
September 29, 1979

✠ FROM THE EUCHARIST SPRINGS THE CHURCH'S mission and capacity to offer her specific contribution to the human family.

The eucharist effectively transmits Christ's parting gift to the world: "Peace I give you, my peace I leave you" (cf. Jn 14:27).

The eucharist is the sacrament of Christ's "peace" because it is the memorial of the salvific redemptive sacrifice of the Cross.

The eucharist is the sacrament of victory over the divisions that flow from personal sin and collective selfishness.

Therefore, the eucharistic community is called to be a model and instrument of a reconciled humanity.

In the Christian community there can be no division, no discrimination, no separation among those who break the bread of life around the one altar of sacrifice.

Homily at Seoul, South Korea,
October 18, 1988

✠ BAPTISM IS THE FIRST AND FUNDAMENTAL consecration of the human person. Beginning a new existence in Christ, the baptized—man or woman—participates in this consecration, in this total donation to the Father which is proper to His eternal Son. It is He Himself—the Son—who incites in man's soul the desire to give oneself without reservation to God: "My soul thirsts for God, for the living God. When shall I come and behold the face of God?" (Ps 42:3).

What Would the World Be Without Consecrated Life?
Homily at Mass, Synod of Bishops, October 29, 1994

✠ THE APOSTLE PAUL SAID: "GOD . . . HAS EN-trusted to us the ministry of reconciliation" (2 Cor 5:18).

The people of God are called to a continual conversion, to an ever renewed reconciliation with God in Christ. This reconciliation is effected in the sacrament of penance, and it is there that you exercise, par excellence, your ministry of reconciliation.

Address to the Priests of Zaire, May 4, 1980

CELIBACY

✠ THE PRIEST WHO, IN THE CHOICE OF CELIBACY, renounces human love to be opened totally to that of God makes himself free to be given to men by a gift excluding no one, but including them all in the flow of charity which comes from God (cf. Rom 5:5) and leads to God. Celibacy, in linking the priest to God, frees him for all the works required by the care of souls.

Address to the Priests of Zaire, May 4, 1980

✠ IN THE LIGHT OF THIS PRINCIPLE SO MANY other aspects of the priesthood are clarified: the value of celibacy is proclaimed, not so much as a practical exigency, but as an expression of a perfect offering and of a configuration to Jesus Christ.

Ad Limina Address to U.S. Bishops, September 9, 1983

WOMEN RELIGIOUS

✠ SINCE THE BEGINNING OF MY PONTIFICATE I have striven to point out the importance of religious consecration in the Church and the value of religious life as it affects the whole community of the faithful. Religious have the task of showing forth the holiness of the whole body of Christ and of bearing witness to a new and eternal life acquired by the redemption of Christ. At the same time they are called to many different apostolates in the Church. Their service in the Gospel is very necessary for the life of the Church.

Address to Bishops, Nairobi, Kenya,
May 29, 1980

✠ YOUR MISSION MIGHT APPEAR TO YOU TO BE too demanding, too big for your capabilities. For you are near the people; in many cases you have the education of children in your hands, the education of young people and adults. By nature and your evangelical mission you have to be sowers of peace and concord, unity and fraternity. You can disconnect the mechanisms of violence through integral education and promoting the authentic values of the person. Your consecrated lives have to be a challenge to egoism and oppression, a call to conversion, a factor of reconciliation among people.

Address to Women Religious, Costa Rica,
March 3, 1983

✠ TO WOMEN RELIGIOUS IS DUE A VERY SPECIAL debt of gratitude for their particular contribution to the field of education. Their authentic educational apostolate was, and is, worthy of the greatest praise. It is an apostolate that requires much self-sacrifice; it is thoroughly human as an expression of religious service; an apostolate that follows closely human and spiritual growth, and accompanies children and young people patiently and lovingly through the problems of youth and the insecurity of adolescence toward Christian maturity.

Address to U.S. Bishops, October 28, 1993

✠ YOUR CONSECRATION BINDS YOU TO THE
Church in a special way; in perfect communion with her,
with her mission, with her pastors and with her faithful,
you will find the full meaning of your religious life. Go on being,
as consecrated women, the honor of mother Church.

Address to Women Religious, Costa Rica, March 3, 1983

✠ PRECISELY THIS FEMININITY — OFTEN CON-
sidered by a certain public opinion as foolishly sacrificed
in religious life — is in fact rediscovered and expanded to a
superior level: that of the kingdom of God.

Address to Women Religious in Zaire, May 3, 1980

CATHOLIC EDUCATION

✠ THE FIRST PRINCIPLE OF THE CHURCH'S SOCIAL
teaching, from which all others derive: the center of the
social order is man, considered in his inalienable dignity
as a creature made "in the image of God." The value of society
comes from the value of man, and not vice versa.

What Church Teaching Is and Is Not, September 9, 1993

✠ MORE THAN EVER, THE CHURCH MUST MAKE ITS
own the words of the apostle: "I am ruined if I do not
preach the gospel!" (1 Cor 9:16).

World Mission Day Message, October 18, 1981

✠ EDUCATORS, YOU HAVE BEEN CONFIDED THE
responsibility to guide the young generations toward an
authentic culture of love, offering yourselves as tutor

and model of faithfulness to the ideal values which give meaning to life.

Address to Vatican AIDS Conference,
November 15, 1989

✠ IN THE HISTORY OF YOUR COUNTRY, AN EXTREMELY
effective instrument of Catholic education has been the Catholic school. It has contributed immensely to the spreading of God's word and has enabled the faithful "to relate human affairs and activities with religious values in a single living synthesis." In the community formed by the Catholic school, the power of the Gospel has been brought to bear on thought patterns, standards of judgment and norms of behavior.

Address to U.S. Bishops,
November 17, 1983

✠ HISTORICALLY, THE CHURCH WAS THE FOUNDER
of universities. For centuries it developed there a conception of the world in which the knowledge of the epoch was situated within the more ample vision of a world created by God and redeemed by our Lord Jesus Christ. Thus, many of its sons consecrated themselves to teaching and research to initiate generations of students into the various degrees of scholarship within a total vision of man, including especially a consideration of the ultimate reasons for his existence.

Address to Zairean Students,
May 29, 1980

✠ AS AN INSTITUTION THE CATHOLIC SCHOOL HAS
to be judged extremely favorably if we apply the sound criterion, "You will know them by their deeds" (Mt 7:16), and again, "You can tell a tree by its fruit" (Mt 7:20). It is easy therefore in the cultural environment of the United States to explain

the wise exhortation contained in the new code: "The faithful are to promote Catholic schools, doing everything possible to help in establishing and maintaining them" (Can. 800:2).

Address to U.S. Bishops,
November 17, 1983

✠ CATHOLIC EDUCATION IN YOUR LAND HAS ALSO fostered numerous vocations over the years. You yourselves owe a great debt of gratitude to that Catholic education which enabled you to understand and to accept the call of the Lord. Among other contributions of Catholic education is the quality of citizens that you were able to produce: upright men and women who contributed to the well-being of America, and through Christian charity worked to serve all their brothers and sisters. Catholic education has furnished an excellent witness to the Church's perennial commitment to culture of every kind. It has exercised a prophetic role—perhaps modestly in individual cases, but overall most effectively—to assist faith to permeate culture. The achievements of Catholic education in America merit our great respect and admiration.

Address to U.S. Bishops,
November 17, 1983

✠ THERE IS STILL, HOWEVER, A DEBT OF GRATITUDE to be paid, before the witness of history, to the parents who have supported a whole system of Catholic education; to the parishes that have coordinated and sustained these efforts; to the dioceses that have promoted programs of education and supplemented means of support, especially in poor areas; to the teachers—who always included a certain number of generous lay men and women—who through dedication and sacrifice championed the cause of helping young people to reach maturity in Christ.

Address to U.S. Bishops,
November 17, 1983

✠ THE CATECHISM IS TRULY GOD'S TIMELY GIFT
to the whole Church and to every Christian at the approach of the new millennium. Indeed, I pray that the Church in the United States will recognize in the catechism an authoritative guide to sound and vibrant preaching, an invaluable resource for parish adult formation programs, a basic text for the upper grade of Catholic high schools, colleges, and universities. The catechism presents in a clear and complete way the riches of the Church's sacramental doctrine based on its genuine sources: Sacred Scripture and tradition as witnessed to by the fathers, doctors and saints, and by the constant teaching of the magisterium.

Ad Limina *Address to the U.S. Bishops of Alabama, Kentucky, Louisiana, Mississippi, and Tennessee, June 5, 1993*

EVIL

✠ REDEMPTION IS ALWAYS GREATER THAN MAN'S
sin and the "sin of the world." The power of the redemption is infinitely superior to the whole range of evil in man and the world.

The Message of Fatima, May 13, 1982

✠ THE CONTRAPOSITION OF GOOD AND EVIL EN-
tered the history of man, destroying the original innocence in the heart of man and woman. "Although set by God in a state of rectitude, man, enticed by the evil one, abused his freedom at the very start of history. He lifted himself up against God and sought to attain his goal apart from Him." From then, "the whole life of men, both individual and social, shows itself to be a struggle, and a dramatic one, between good and evil, between light and darkness. For sin brought man to a lower state,

forcing him away from the completeness that is his to attain"
(*Gaudium et Spes*, 13).

Homily at Opening Mass, Synod of Bishops,
September 29, 1983

ECUMENISM

✠ TRUE PEACE CAN EXIST ONLY ON THE BASIS OF A
process of unification in which each people is able to
choose, in freedom and truth, the paths of its own development. Moreover, such a process is impossible if there is no
agreement on the original and fundamental unity which is manifested in different forms, not opposed but complementary, which
need one another and seek one another.

Euntes in Mundum (Go into All the World)

✠ IN THESE MOMENTS FULL OF JOY AND AFTER
having the experience of a profound spiritual communion
which we desire to share with the pastors and the faithful
as much of the East as of the West, we lift up our hearts toward
Him who is the head, Christ. It is from Him that the entire body
receives concord and cohesion, thanks to all the members who
serve it by an activity shared according to the capacity of each.
Thus the body realizes its natural growth. Thus, the body con-
structs itself in love (cf. Eph 4:16).

Joint Declaration of Pope John Paul II and Patriarch Dimitrios I,
December 7, 1987

✠ THE CHURCHES OF THE EAST AND THE WEST,
over the centuries, have celebrated together the ecumenical councils which have proclaimed and defended "the

faith which was once for all handed down to the holy ones" (Jude 3). "Called to the one hope" (Eph 4:4), we wait for the day desired by God when the rediscovered unity in the faith will be celebrated and when full communion will be reestablished by a concelebration of the eucharist of the Lord.

Joint Declaration of Pope John Paul II and Patriarch Dimitrios I,
December 7, 1987

THE ARTS

✠ EVERY PIECE OF ART, BE IT RELIGIOUS OR SECU-lar, be it a painting, a sculpture, a poem or any form of handicraft made by loving skill, is a sign and a symbol of the inscrutable secret of human existence, of man's origin and destiny, of the meaning of his life and work. It speaks to us of the meaning of birth and death, of the greatness of man.

Address at Clonmacnoise, Ireland,
September 30, 1979

✠ FOR A LONG TIME, THE CHURCH WAS CONSID-ered the mother of the arts. It was the Church which com-missioned art. The contents of Christian faith determined the motifs and themes of art. How true this is can easily be demonstrated by stopping to think what would remain if one re-moved everything connected with religious and Christian inspi-ration from European and German art history. In recent centuries, most strongly since about 1800, the connection be-tween the Church and culture, and thus between the Church and art, has grown more tenuous.

Address at Munich,
November 19, 1980

✠ TODAY, LITERATURE, THE THEATER, FILM AND
the visual arts see their function largely in terms of criticism, protest, opposition and pointing an accusing finger at existing conditions. The beautiful as a category of art seems to have fallen by the wayside in favor of depictions of man in his negative aspects, in his contradictions, in his hopelessness and in the absence of meaning. This seems to be the current *ecce homo*. The so-called intact world is an object of scorn and cynicism.

Address at Munich, November 19, 1980

EASTER

✠ THIS IS THE DAY THAT THE LORD HAS MADE FOR
us. The day of a great testimony and a great challenge. The day of God's great response to man's unceasing questions. Questions about man, his origin and his destiny, about the meaning and dimension of his existence. This is the day the Lord has made for us. "Christ, our Paschal lamb, has been sacrificed" (1 Cor 5:7). "Pasch" means passing. The passing of God through human history. Passing through the inevitability of human death, which from the beginning and until the end is the gate to eternity. Passing through the history of human sin, which in God's heart is man's death: passing to life in God.

Easter Message, March 30, 1986

✠ "THIS IS THE DAY THAT THE LORD HAS MADE"
(Ps 118:24). This day ever reconfirms this truth for us: God does not "resign" Himself to man's death. Christ came into the world to convince it of this. Christ died on the cross and was placed in the tomb to bear witness precisely to this fact: God does not "resign" Himself to man's death. For He "is not God of the dead, but of the living" (Mt 22:32). In Christ death has been

defied. Christ by His death has conquered death. Behold the day which the Lord has made. This is the day of God's great uprising: His uprising against death.

The last word of God on the human condition is not death but life; not despair but hope. To this hope the Church invites the men and women of today as well. She repeats to them the incredible but true proclamation: Christ is risen! Let the whole world rise with Him! Alleluia!

Easter Message, March 30, 1986

ACKNOWLEDGMENTS

The editors would like to thank Christopher Lee, Thomas Kelly, and especially Anna Bonta for their research assistance. We were particularly fortunate in having Father John White as an adviser on theological points in the manuscript, as the author of a superb introduction to this volume, and, most important, as a friend. We acknowledge the publishing contribution of St. Paul Books and Media, which publishes all the encyclicals, apostolic letters, and other documents of the Vatican and Pope John Paul II at very reasonable prices. We are also indebted to Father Jude of St. Hyacinth Seminary, Beverly Wilson of the St. Hyacinth Seminary Library, and Sister Regina Melican of St. Joseph's Seminary Library for their assistance in gathering material. And we owe a particular debt of gratitude to the Libreria Editrice Vaticana for allowing us to reprint the Pope's words.

Karen Levine and John Loudon of HarperCollins San Francisco have been extremely diligent in helping us at each stage of the development of this book, for which we are extremely grateful.

BIBLIOGRAPHY

The following bibliography is by no means complete or systematic, but it provides the reader with readily available English renderings in book form of the encyclicals, many important apostolic letters and apostolic exhortations, plus hundreds of speeches, sermons, and addresses. Almost all the Pope's speeches are published in periodicals, especially in the Vatican's *Osservatore Romano*, a weekly edition of which is published in English (as well as in many other languages), and in *The Pope Speaks*, a bimonthly magazine published by Our Sunday Visitor, Inc.

Apostolic Letter of His Holiness Pope John Paul II on the Christian Meaning of Human Suffering. St. Paul Editions, Boston, 1984.

Be Not Afraid: John Paul II Speaks Out on His Life, His Beliefs, and His Inspiring Vision for Humanity. St. Martin's Press, New York, 1984.

Blessed Are the Pure of Heart: Catechesis on the Sermon on the Mount and the Writings of St. Paul. St. Paul Editions, Boston, 1983.

Brazil, Journey in the Light of the Eucharist: Sermons. St. Paul Editions, Boston, 1980.

The Collected Plays and Writings on Theater. University of California Press, Berkeley and Los Angeles, 1987.

Covenant of Love: Pope John Paul II on Sexuality, Marriage, and Family in the Modern World. Doubleday, Garden City, NY, 1985.

Draw Near to God. Servant Books, Ann Arbor, MI, 1987.

Encyclical Letter "Dives in Misericordia" of the Supreme Pontiff John Paul II on the Mercy of God. St. Paul Editions, Boston, 1981.

Essays on Religious Freedom. Catholic League for Religious and Civil Rights, Milwaukee, 1984.

Evangelium Vitae. St. Paul Editions, Boston, 1995.

The Family: Center of Love and Life. Compiled and indexed by the Daughters of St. Paul. St. Paul Editions, Boston, 1981.

The Far East Journey of Peace and Brotherhood. St. Paul Editions, Boston, 1981.

France: Message of Peace, Trust, Love, and Faith. St. Paul Editions, Boston, 1980.

Fruitful and Responsible Love. Seabury Press, New York, 1979.

Germany: Pilgrimage of Unity and Peace. St. Paul Editions, Boston, 1981.

The Gospel of Life, the Papal Encyclical "Evangelium Vitae." In *Origins: CNS Documentary Service*, April 6, 1995.

I Believe in Youth, Christ Believes in Youth: To the Young People of the World. St. Paul Editions, Boston, 1981.

John Paul II and the Laity. Le Jacq Publishers, 1984.

John Paul II for Peace in the Middle East. Libreria Editrice Vaticana, Vatican City, 1992.

Letter of the Supreme Pontiff, Pope John Paul II, to All the Bishops of the Church on the Mystery of the Eucharist. St. Paul Editions, Boston, 1980.

Lord and Giver of Life: Encyclical Letter "Dominum et Vivificantem" of the Supreme Pontiff John Paul II on the Holy Spirit in the Life of the Church and the World. U.S. Catholic Conference, Washington, DC, 1986.

Marian Reflections: The Angelus Messages of Pope John Paul II. AMI Press, Washington, DC, 1990.

On Human Work, Encyclical "Laborem Exercens." St. Paul Editions, Boston, 1981.

Original Unity of Man and Woman: Catechesis on the Book of Genesis. St. Paul Editions, Boston, 1981.

Person and Community: Selected Essays. P. Lang Publishers, New York, 1993.

Pilgrimage of Peace: The Collected Speeches of John Paul II in Ireland and the United States. Farrar, Straus & Giroux, New York, 1980.

Pilgrim to Poland: Sermons. St. Paul Editions, Boston, 1979.

The Pope and Revolution: John Paul II Confronts Liberation Theology. Ethics and Public Policy Center, Washington, DC, 1982.

Pope John Paul II on Jews and Judaism: 1979–1986. U.S. Catholic Conference, Washington, DC, 1987.

The Pope Speaks to the American Church: John Paul's Homilies, Speeches, and Letters to Catholics in the United States. HarperCollins, San Francisco, 1992.

Prayers and Devotions from Pope John Paul II: Selected Passages from His Writings and Speeches Arranged for Every Day of the Year. Regnery Gateway, Chicago, 1984.

Reflections on Humanae Vitae: Conjugal Morality and Spirituality. St. Paul Editions, Boston, 1984.

Sacred in All Its Forms. St. Paul Editions, Boston, 1984.

Second Pastoral Visit of His Holiness Pope John Paul II to the United States of America. Catholic Book Publishing Co., New York, 1987.

Sign of Contradiction. Seabury Press, New York, 1979.

Sources of Renewal: The Implementation of the Second Vatican Council. Harper & Row, San Francisco, 1980.

Talks of John Paul II. Compiled by the Daughters of St. Paul. St. Paul Editions, Boston, 1979.

Through the Priestly Ministry, the Gift of Salvation: Messages of John Paul II to Bishops, Priests, and Deacons. St. Paul Editions, Boston, 1982.

Through the Year with Pope John Paul II: Readings for Every Day of the Year. Crossroad, New York, 1981.

To the U.S. Bishops at Their Ad Limina Visits: April 15–December 3, 1983. St. Paul Editions, Boston, 1981.